Rock Gardening

Rock Gardening

Reimagining
a Classic Style

JOSEPH TYCHONIEVICH

Timber Press
Portland, Oregon

Contents

Introduction

A warm welcome to
the fascinating miniature
world of gardening
among rocks.

**No other kind
of garden
offers as many
opportunities for
experimentation
and enjoyment
as a rock garden.**

Rock gardening, the art of growing alpines
and other miniature plants—often in the
company of rocks to recreate the look of
a rugged mountaintop—has been surging
in popularity. There are many reasons
that this classic design is coming back into ▶

left › *Aquilegia canadensis* on a cliff-face in western North Carolina.

below › *Anemonella thalictroides* blooming on a stone in Atlanta, Georgia.

right › *Asperula suberosa* showing the classic beauty of an alpine plant.

style. Gardeners today generally have less time and less space to garden than their parents or grandparents did, while rock gardening allows an urban gardener with an apartment balcony or tiny plot to grow a bewildering diversity of different plants in a small space, and maintenance takes a fraction of the time required to deal with a similar number of plants in a large perennial border. In addition, many rock garden plants are notably tolerant of—or even fond of—dry conditions, making them the perfect answer to the chronic droughts that seem to be becoming the new normal in much of the American West and elsewhere.

Aesthetics is driving people to rock gardens as well. As with anything else, from fashion to food, we get tired of the familiar and want fresh, exciting approaches. The spare, architectural forms and dramatic flowering of alpines are in stark contrast to and a welcome change from the lush containers of annuals and thickly planted perennial beds that have dominated gardening trends for so long. Add to that the fad for fairy gardening, which makes use of tiny plants but with a heavy dose of bright, exuberant,

above › **A traditional rock garden at Royal Botanic Garden Edinburgh, Scotland.**

right › *Allium schoenoprasum*, *Jasione montana,* and *Daucus carota* growing on cliffs on the Lizard Peninsula, Cornwall.

above right › **From plant choices to design, this southwestern garden looks little like a traditional rock garden, yet it is based on the same gardening principles.**

over-the-top fantasy notably lacking from traditionalist rock gardens (traditionalists being fond of their rules and their proper ways of doing things), and, well, you've got a perfect storm: a new wave of rock gardeners and gardens that are beautiful, exciting, and fresh.

This new trend in rock gardening is part of a long aesthetic tradition that starts with scenes that anyone who hikes around mountains or cliffs or stony ground will know well: a ridge, cliff-face, or big boulder with plants tucked down in a crevice between two stones, in the soil behind a rock, or even in a shallow pocket of leaf mold collecting in a stony depression. The visual effect of a delicate, beautiful flower set against the hard austerity of stone provides a dramatic contrast, and there is something magical about a seemingly fragile columbine or lewisia managing not just to live but also to thrive in what appears to be a hostile, lifeless location.

Rock gardening starts with that image of beauty amid rocks, and draws the bulk of its inspiration from the harsh conditions at the tops of mountains where there is an abundance of stony crevices and striking plants specialized to live among them. Plants in these high alpine regions tend to evolve in a very distinctive, beautiful way. Exposed to harsh winds, limited water, and fierce sun, they tend to stay extremely small and compact, forming tight mounds that can withstand the brutality of the climate. At

the same time, these harsh conditions mean that pollinating insects like bees can be few and far between; so when it is time to reproduce, plants go all out, producing huge numbers of often wildly disproportionately large flowers to make sure they draw in every potential pollinator in the area. The result is what I think of as the classic alpine plant—a tiny, dense mound of leaves that can completely cover itself in a solid sheet of brilliant flowers.

Enjoying the simple beauty of plants against rocks, and cultivating the distinctive forms of alpine plants, is the heart of traditional rock gardening, ranging from gardeners who obsessively recreate the look of mountaintops, to those who carefully cultivate individual specimens of plants into breathtaking peaks of bloom not to be matched by anything else in the plant world.

But from that old-school rocks-and-alpines version, rock gardening has been evolving. Traditional rock gardening has moved out to different parts

of the world, taking on different forms as gardeners explore and adapt to their local conditions and tastes. Many plants native to dry, desert areas are just as happy in well-drained gardens as alpines are, and look just as lovely against a rock. So particularly in the American West, you are as likely to see cacti and agaves in a rock garden as the more traditional alpine dianthus and saxifrages. And traditional rock garden plants don't have to be grown with rocks: a subtle layer of sand and gravel added in parts of the perennial border can make for perfect conditions to grow alpines in what may not look much like a traditional rock garden at all.

left › **Matchbox cars add a note of the gleefully absurd to Baldassare Mineo's Oregon garden.**

Gardeners with a lot of shade have been taking rock gardening in yet another direction, finding that plants like miniature hostas, heucheras, and asarums are both very happy and look great growing between stones in a shady rockery, even though they are not true alpine plants.

This book aims to be an introduction into that wide world of the rock garden in all its diverse modern incarnations. To that end, we'll start with a series of garden tours, visits to gardens across the United States and the

above › *Viola pedata* blooming in a trough at Paula Flynn's Iowa garden is the sophisticated aesthetic opposite of a loud pot full of petunias and coleus.

United Kingdom to show you the full range of diversity within rock gardening, and give you ideas and inspiration for rock gardens you might want to create. With that inspiration in mind, the second section moves to the practical how-to, delving into the techniques and methods specific to creating and maintaining a rock garden—ranging from dealing with the vagaries of your local climate to choosing the right soil. The final section is a tour through some of the classic rock garden plants, especially those suitable for beginners, so you can start assembling a palette of terrific plants for your first rock garden or renew your love affair with the rock garden you already have.

Gardens

Looking up at the rock garden, the different levels displaying tiny plants to perfection.

My number one goal in writing this book was to go big and broad, not merely to write about how I rock garden in my specific climate here ▶

in Michigan, but rather to open a window into the full breadth of this form of gardening.

So I got on planes, rented cars, and visited gardens all over the United States and United Kingdom to try and capture how rock gardening looks and works in as many different climates and regions as possible.

The differences in climate were fascinating and illuminating. I grow daphnes by putting them in a raised bed full of sand and never watering them; in Medford, Oregon, they have to be irrigated; and in Scotland I saw them growing under glass roofs to keep the excess rain off. Perhaps even more fascinating was to see how different styles of gardening can be. Two gardens in the very same region, growing largely the same plants, can be utterly different, some focusing on the plants, some on beautiful stonework, some naturalistic, and others whimsical and playful.

As different as every garden I chose to profile is, they are all relatively small, intimate, and personal—mostly private gardens created by gardeners like you. Though I saw some truly impressive rock gardens on massive scales (Royal Botanic Garden Edinburgh, I'm looking at you), I chose not to focus on them in this section of garden profiles for one simple reason. As you flip through the profiles that follow and see an image of a garden that you love, I want you to know that you can create something similar in your own garden. These aren't gardens that require a staff of hundreds, or vast acreage, or moving in a small mountain range's worth of stone. These are gardens to inspire you to get out and create your own perfect rock garden.

In addition to selecting smaller gardens, I've tried to make these garden profiles more than just a collection of pretty pictures by including practical takeaways from each garden, be they design ideas, techniques, or concepts. So this section not only fosters dreams of beautiful gardens, but also helps you make those dreams a reality.

Branklyn Garden

Pulling out all the stops in a small space

Color echoes in shrubs large and small around a path to an inviting bench.

All the traveling and visiting of gardens I've done for this book has generally had the effect of making me appreciate more and more where I garden in Michigan and the plants that thrive in my climate at home. Because although everywhere I go I see lots of plants doing exceptionally well, far better than they've ever grown for me, right next to them are plants that are easy ▶

and vigorous in my climate limping along rather pitifully. It has driven home the point to me that there is no perfect climate, no magical location where you can grow all the plants better; it's rather a matter of finding the perfect plants for where you are and growing them so well you reduce visitors to fits of jealousy.

Except, that is, for Branklyn. This place may well be the perfect climate, and lodged somewhere deep in my heart now is the feeling that nowhere I'll ever live is going to be quite as nice. True, their daphnes weren't as vigorous as they are back home in Michigan, but oh my, everything else—it is a breathtaking place, with plants grown to absolute perfection.

Started in 1922, Branklyn was created as the private garden of John and Dorothy Renton. And now, under the auspices of the National Trust of Scotland, you can visit this magnificent little garden and go home with a massive dose of inspiration for just a few pounds. This is a garden you can take notes in and come away with ideas and insights, partly, I think, because it is not a large garden, but rather an intimate one. Unlike, say, the Royal Botanic Garden Edinburgh, which has a truly massive rock garden built on an imposing scale that simply doesn't translate to a home garden unless

left › **A bench invites visitors to sit and enjoy the garden in bloom.**

below › **A path leads you through the rock gardens and on to the beauties beyond.**

right › **The Branklyn house with the rock garden spilling down below it.**

Embracing brief beauty

So often when flipping through a garden book or catalog, we get presented with more and more plants that bloom all summer long, and these long-performing plants obviously have much to recommend them. And while I wouldn't want a rock garden without the continuous bloom of a plant like *Daphne jasminea*, I also don't think that plants like the dwarf rhododendrons at Branklyn, which pull out all the stops for one stunning but short-lived display, should be given any less respect and attention. Far from being a flaw, intense seasonal bloom is a feature I love in the garden. Sure, I appreciate the steady, pretty flowers of *Gypsophila repens* pumping out all summer long, but they never quite leave me weak at the knees and running for my camera the way

Primula allionii 'Superba'.

a perfect clump of *Primula allionii* in brief, perfect, full bloom does. A garden isn't meant to be practical: it is supposed to thrill you. So indulge in planting a whole bed to come into riotous bloom for just one week in May. Anticipate it, long for it, throw a party in its honor, and enjoy it for all it's worth.

you have an estate and staff and money to burn, Branklyn is only 2 acres in total. It's full of small, intimate plantings that could easily be imitated at home even if your garden is much smaller (perhaps with some adjustment of the particular species used, depending on your location).

Branklyn clearly has a nice supply of acidic soil, and they use this to make a wide array of rhododendrons, from the larger shrubs down to small, alpine species, very happy, along with many other ericaceous plants. They

Rhododendrons and Japanese maples make a quiet corner for a Japanese stone lantern.

left › *Anemone ranunculoides* and *Omphalodes cappadocica* 'Cherry Ingram'.

below left › Branklyn rock garden with *Rhododendron* 'Golden Bee' in the foreground.

below › The house and conifers both provide structure around the rock garden.

further support these acid-loving plants by using peat blocks to build up raised beds. These solid blocks, cut from the peat bog (not to be confused with the compressed blocks of peat which have first been ground and then packed into a block shape), are at once structural, supporting the soil of the raised beds, and also a growing surface, perfect homes for many acid-loving small plants.

You enter the garden through a little gate, pay your entry fee, walk past the beautiful old house, and then go down into the main rock garden: a little pool of sun with beautiful plants from armerias to dwarf rhododendrons tucked between shadier parts of the garden, where the larger rhododendrons, Japanese maples, and other shrubs and small trees grow.

As you move past the main rock garden, you still get bits of small, alpine-like plants scattered elsewhere; like pockets of heather in bloom echoing the purple shades of a larger rhododendron behind it, or a shady rock garden where yellow *Anemone ranunculoides* blooms next to the rich, true blue of *Omphalodes cappadocica* 'Cherry Ingram'.

Aysgarth Edwardian Rock Garden

NORTH YORKSHIRE, ENGLAND

Antique style worth rediscovering

A bench below a tapestry of stones and *Bergenia cordifolia*, *Armeria maritima*, and *Campanula garganica* 'Dickson's Gold'.

Aysgarth is a piece of rock gardening history. Built from 1906 to 1914 for the original owner, Frank Sayer Graham, it passed through many hands before eventually being left to get swallowed up by weedy trees and brambles. Until 2002, that is, when Angela and Peter Jauneika set upon the monumental task of cleaning it up and restoring the garden to its former ▶

Hellebores
blooming among
the rocks.

above right ›
*Armeria
maritima* and
*Campanula
garganica*
'Dickson's Gold'.

right › **A tiny fairy
adds a note of
whimsy.**

glory, a task now carried on by the current owners, Adrian and Rosemary Anderson. The result is a time capsule of a garden, harkening back to an earlier style of rock garden that really is worth bringing back.

The look of this garden is so different because it was created before the incredibly influential botanist and rock gardener Reginald Farrer revolutionized rock gardening and established the aesthetic ideals that have dominated rock gardening ever since. Farrer had been rock gardening since his teens, but in his early twenties, in 1902, he took an eight-month trip to East Asia, where the Japanese gardening style based on an idealized version of natural forms inspired him to rethink English rock gardening. Instead of creating whimsical and clearly artificial structures, he pioneered a naturalistic approach based on laying stones to mimic the patterns and formations found in natural rock. When he presented this design vision in his hugely popular book, *My Rock-Garden,* he established the style that remains dominant today, more than 100 years later.

But Aysgarth is built in the style of gardens pre-Farrer, and is a full on Edwardian folly. Rather than being based on an idealized version of nature, this garden is a fully—perhaps even gleefully—artificial fantasy with stones built up in wild sudden cliffs and mountains, and little tunnels and grottos that never, even for a moment, could you imagine might have arrived

The delicate beauty of *Primula rosea* perfectly set off by rugged rock.

The waterfall, with *Primula denticulata* scattered among the rocks.

without the hand of man. I'll confess, hearing it described I didn't think I would like it, because I've seen many a rock garden that failed by looking artificial when it was trying to look naturalistic—but I loved Aysgarth. The secret to Aysgarth's success, I think, is in fully embracing its wild fantasy look. No apologies, no failed attempts at naturalism: it works. And maybe this style of rock garden is due for a comeback: naturalism is wonderful, but other aesthetics are worth exploring as well. I think this style is perfectly suited to gardeners who are coming to rocks and alpines by way of fairy gardening. One tiny fairy, in fact, situated in the garden looked perfectly in place in this fantasyland; other miniature props that might look silly in a naturalistic design would be perfectly at home in this garden.

The wild stone structure of the garden has been carefully planted with a wide range of plants, some used in surprising ways. Perhaps most strikingly, one of the tall rock crags is topped with a great colony of bergenias, which usually grow in cool, shady spots. But they are quite well adapted to growing in rocky crevices, particularly in cooler climates like much of the United Kingdom and the northern United States. As an added bonus, while slugs love bergenias, they hate exposed, rocky places, so siting the plants

above › **Masses
of stone, with
bergenia at the top.**

left › **Stones piled
high frame the
view.**

Going up

Building up in the style of Aysgarth is not only a fascinating aesthetic approach; you can also use it to create radically different microclimates for your garden. A steep grade of rock facing south or west will bask in the sun during the warmest parts of the day, absorbing heat that the stones will hold into the night to create a significantly warmer microclimate. This is particularly useful for gardeners in cool areas trying to make good homes for rock garden plants from lower, drier, altitudes like some bulbs, cacti, and penstemons that prefer a warm summer. On the other side, facing north or east, the rock will provide shade during the heat of the day for a cool microclimate. By building up around that cool side with more stone to block harsh winds, and adding a small stream splashing down over and between the rocks, you can create a little haven of cool, humid air—essential for gardeners in hot, dry climates who want to cultivate species like many of the Asian gentians or delicate woodland blue corydalis.

there should minimize slug damage. Heucheras would love it there as well, along with—if you give them a bit of afternoon shade—hostas.

A very cool thing about the sheer scale of the rock structures in this garden is that it produces hugely varied microclimates. Hot, dry, south-facing sides make perfect sites for sun-lovers like armeria and aubrieta, while the cool, shadier grotto near the spray of the waterfall is a totally different habitat for masses of *Primula denticulata*. This difference is particularly dramatic because the garden is tiny; only 0.14 acre, it is as small as all but the smallest of home gardens. But by building upward so vigorously, they've created a multitude of garden areas and quite simply a lot more surface area and room to plant than if the garden had been left flat.

So maybe it is time to consider getting a bunch of stone and constructing a narrow, 20-foot mountain in your back garden. No, it won't look natural, but it will look amazing. And will be a lot of fun.

Stones built up into a soaring cliff-face.

Ev Whittemore

Uncompromising beauty without heavy lifting

Sempervivums around one of the garden houses.

Ev Whittemore's garden is built on a steep slope tucked into the mountains of western North Carolina. Driving to visit her garden had me winding through curving roads and finally up to her charming little house perched on the edge of a steep hill. The garden itself is built, without terraces, on this hillside. The steep lay of the land is perfect for growing many ▶

above › **The long view up the hillside.**

right › **Carefully placed dianthus blooming in the gravel walk.**

alpine plants of course, as excess water drains away quickly, and it allows all the plants at different levels to be visible at once without being blocked or shaded by those in front of them. The sunny part of the hill—the bulk of her garden—is a giant sweep of gravel mulch with relatively few rocks, along with the occasional container and simple sculptures.

At the base of the hill, where the garden becomes shady, she switches to bark mulch and a sampling of shade-loving miniature plants as well as a few troughs. At the top of the hill she has her small vegetable garden and a little bog garden planted up with pitcher plants, bog cranberries, and a splash of true, clear, sky blue in the flowers of *Houstonia caerulea*.

If there were one word to describe Ev's garden, it would be immaculate. There is not a weed to be seen, not a bit of mulch out of place, and every plant is grown to absolute perfection: lush, happy, and in exactly the right spot. It is also entirely handmade. This is not a garden with a staff or a team of people hired in to build it for her. The troughs she made herself from hypertufa, which is not that unusual, but what was more surprising

Epimedium grandiflorum 'White Queen' in the shady rock garden.

Adding bogs

Though the constantly wet conditions of a bog are in some ways the polar opposite of the sharp drainage of the rock garden, bog gardens are easy to create and provide ideal habitat for a host of unusual and striking small plants that will complement a traditional rock garden beautifully. Natural bogs form where plentiful water keeps the ground saturated and leaches away nearly all the nutrients to create lean, acidic conditions. To recreate these conditions in your garden, use a pond liner or a container without drainage holes, fill it with peat, and keep it topped up with very pure water like rainwater or distilled

water. (An easy source of distilled water for many people is what drips from the air conditioner.) Then add some of the amazing carnivorous plant species: pitcher plants (*Sarracenia* species), hardy sundews (*Drosera* species), and of course Venus fly trap (*Dionaea muscipula*), all of which are easy and winter-hardy to zone 6. Add a few great flowers in the form of bluet (*Houstonia caerulea*) or a bottle gentian like *Gentiana catesbaei*, and you'll have a very worthwhile bog to enjoy in your rock garden.

Houstonia caerulea in the bog.

above › *Sarracenia* blooming in a bog container.

Hypertufa stone
getting a spray
paint treatment
before going into
the garden.

to me—surprising enough that I didn't notice it at all until she pointed it out—is that even most of the "rocks" in her garden are handmade. Some of them are old troughs that were broken and repurposed as garden stones, but far more are simply pieces of hypertufa she's made specifically for a certain location in the garden or to embellish the container plantings.

Building her own stones gives her exactly the size and look she wants for a specific location, while being incredibly economical and significantly lighter and easier to move than real rocks. She can haul them around the garden and put them in place herself (not a small consideration for this fiercely independent woman). Hypertufa develops a very natural look with age as it gets colonized with mosses and lichen, but Ev jump-starts the process with spray paint. Yes, spray paint. And it works wonders. She makes it look far easier than it is, but with a little experimentation you can get the technique down as well. First she puts down a light coat of black and then follows with ever-so-gentle touches of red and green. The final result is an impressively natural, aged-looking stone that looks entirely at home in the garden.

In addition to making stones and troughs with hypertufa, she makes little houses as well. Though one could call them fairy houses I suppose,

above › **Looking up the hillside, neatly mulched with bright gravel.**

they look more like little adobe pueblos. Their form is subtle and under-stated, and blends gracefully into the landscape.

Ev's garden is full of notes that look careless and naturalistic, but they are actually highly contrived. Her bog garden, planted with native species, is entirely naturalistic in effect, but she created it by adding a rubber pond liner to hold water and create the bog conditions these plants demand. Similarly, in the sweep of smooth gravel in front of her house, there are a few dianthus blooming in solid sheets of pink flowers that look as if they just

happened to seed in here and there in the gravel. Nothing could be further from the truth: they are sitting in special planting pockets of good soil she put there just for them, carefully arranged and placed to look as if they just happened along.

Coming away from Ev's garden, I took some lessons on gardening back with me. One of them is not to be afraid of space. My instinct is to jam as many plants into the garden as possible, but she leaves open spaces and stretches of gravel or bark mulch between individual specimens and planting combinations, and these open spaces set off the plants to great effect.

The other thing I carried away was an utmost respect for her energy and drive. The steep hillside garden, the handmade containers and stones, the perfectly spread mulch—all that takes a lot of energy! The moment I'll always remember is Ev, a slightly built, white-haired woman of over 80 years, looking at her nearly vertical garden and commenting that it isn't quite as easy as it used to be to haul wheelbarrow loads of gravel up and down the hills. I'm guessing most people would blanch at the idea of hauling rocks up or down that hill—when they were a quarter of her age. That is an extra benefit of being a rock gardener: it keeps you young. Ev isn't slowing down one bit. And I fully intend to follow her example.

right › **Alpines, including** *Lewisia cotyledon* **and** *Erigeron scopulorum,* **in the crevices of one of Ev's homemade hypertufa rocks.**

Glenn Shapiro

LANCASHIRE, ENGLAND

Turning a liability into an asset

Saxifrages in a
rock crevice.

Immediately behind Glenn's beautiful old
stone house rises a dramatic limestone
cliff with every niche and crevice planted
up with glorious alpine plants, creating an
effect that is dramatic and stunning.
But when she arrived there in the 1980s
and set out to make a garden, it looked
anything but appealing. Directly behind
the house was a hog pen, where today ▶

above › Glenn's house as seen from the top of the rock garden.

right › *Hepatica* 'Hazelwood Froggie' selected and named by Glenn.

center › The edge of the pond makes a home for wet-loving plants, including *Caltha palustris*.

Omphalodes forms lush pools of rich, true-blue flowers. And the lovely stone cliff was covered in a layer of rubbish that had been pitched over the hog fence for years, topped off by a mass of brush and brambles. Perhaps other gardeners would have concluded that the nearly vertical stone cliff was not the place for a garden, and limited themselves to the flat ground at its base, but Glenn saw the landscape with a rock gardener's eye. In that rough, natural wall of stone she saw not a problem but an opportunity. So she set to clearing the brush and rubbish and started planting away. The results are enough to make any gardener wish they could trade their fertile, level, stone-free ground for a rugged cliff.

Though her garden is defined by the natural stone structure, Glenn has artfully augmented here and there by stacking rocks to form low walls to hold a little more soil and adding a pond and stream. When I visited, the pump for the water was turned off to preserve the developing tadpoles, but most of the year it flows in channels between the stones, forming three

Saxifrages and sedums planted in an island named after a grandchild.

above › The stone
slabs of the
cliffside make a
perfect backdrop
for blooming
saxifrages.

right › *Fritillaria
meleagris* at the
base of the rock
garden.

above › **Aubrieta**
in bloom with
lily-of-the-valley
in a crevice.

left › *Tulipa*
saxatilis **in a level**
area of the rocky
cliff garden.

HOW TO PLANT A STRAWBERRY POT

Strawberry pots are a fine way to grow many alpines, not just hepaticas, as they offer probably the easiest way to create the right conditions for plants that like to grow on steep hillsides or cliff-faces. One huge advantage to them in wet, rainy climates is that by holding the plant on its side, they prevent water from collecting in tight rosettes, so they are particularly useful for growing plants like lewisia, carduncellus, and *Saxifraga longifolia*.

1 Choose your plants with the pot in mind. Aesthetically, any fairly tight-growing bun like a dianthus or trailing form like *Gentiana septemfida* will look great growing out of the side of a strawberry pot. Limiting yourself to just one species or variety per pot will make for a more elegant look. More upright growers, like auricula primroses, might look odd, as they'll try and turn themselves upright rather than tumbling down. Be aware that it can be difficult to remove a large, mature plant from a strawberry pot once it has grown into it, so avoid shrubs like daphnes, dwarf conifers, and other larger growers that will need to be moved up in a few years.

2 To plant, use a well-drained potting medium, mixing in extra sand or gravel as needed for drainage.

3 Fill the strawberry pot with soil up to each hole, slide your plant in, and continue filling in with more soil. If the root ball is too big to slide through the opening in the pot, gently shake off extra soil until it will fit through.

Hepatica in a strawberry pot.

Omphalodes in the former hog pen.

distinct islands in the stream, each island named for one of her grandchildren. More excavation may be on the way: a fourth grandchild is expected. So Glenn is either going to have to create a new island or decide on another garden feature as a namesake.

The bedrock here is all limestone, so of course the soil in her garden is highly alkaline. She could—as one of her neighbors does—augment with peat to create acidic planting pockets to accommodate acid-loving rhododendrons and the like. But Glenn's approach is to go with what she's got naturally, and the lack of acidic soil certainly doesn't seem to have limited the garden anyway—the saxifrages and other lime lovers are utterly happy and beautiful.

One might think that a garden built on a limestone cliff-face would be difficult to maintain, but Glenn says the opposite is true. She has traditional perennial borders on the level ground above the rock wall, and since she had a knee replaced, has had to hire occasional help to keep on top of it. The rock garden, however, is much easier and she still maintains it entirely herself. The paths are smooth and gentle, winding their way up the stone, and with everything growing in spaces between the rocks, there is far less bending down involved in weeding, planting, and maintaining. It proves the point I've often argued: rock gardens are the perfect option for people who lack the time or energy to maintain a large, traditional perennial border—you can pack so much interest into a small space and easily raise things up to your level rather than always having to bend down to the plants.

In addition to her rock garden, Glenn's other great passion is her collection of hepaticas. Though not strictly alpine plants, these little woodland perennials—which are native all over the Northern Hemisphere—like to grow on steep hillsides with absolutely perfect drainage, so revel in rock garden conditions in the shade. Glenn holds a national collection of hepaticas; she has a huge alpine house filled with perfectly grown specimens

right › **The rock garden seen from below.**

below › **Glenn's hepatica collection.**

from Europe, Asia, and the United States with a myriad different colors and flower forms, often with lovely patterned foliage. She also grows them about in shady corners of the garden in containers, especially—and beautifully—in strawberry pots. It was unexpected to me, seeing a hepatica spilling out of the side of a strawberry pot, but growing them this way is frankly brilliant, nearly perfectly mimicking the cliffside habitats where hepaticas are found in the wild. Seeing how happily the hepaticas grow there makes me want to plant up a whole bunch of strawberry pots with alpines—surely lewisias and saxifrages would be just as delighted to grow in those conditions.

Glenn's gorgeous garden is a perfect example of not just adapting to but reveling in what you've got. Steep, stony, alkaline ground would send many a gardener running in terror. Glenn has turned that "problem" into one of the most exciting gardens I've ever seen.

Helen Nelson

DENVER, COLORADO

Intricate beauty on a suburban scale

A tapestry of spring bloom.

Denver, Colorado, is rock gardening heaven. It is, really, enough to make you sick. The high elevation and low humidity ensure that temperatures drop every evening, giving alpine plants the cool nights they love, followed up with bright, clear sunshine needed to grow the tightest buns and domes. Lewisias, which I can grow, but not well, seed around Denver ▶

above left › **A silver sheet of *Arenaria tetraquetra* with pink billows of *Asperula suberosa* behind it.**

above center › Helen's front garden in riotous bloom.

left › Soft gray, white, and pink dominate, contrasting perfectly with the warmer tones of the stone.

gardens like weeds—did I mention it is enough to make you sick sometimes? Denver's one weakness, of course, is lack of water. Not much falls from the sky, and irrigation relies on massive pipes bringing water from the other side of the mountains. But with a rapidly growing population and changing climate, that could be running out. We'll see what the future holds, but currently they have water on tap and virtually none falling from the sky, so Denver gardeners are able to give plants just the amount they want, rather than cursing fruitlessly at cloudy, rainy skies the way I do.

As delightful as some aspects of Denver's climate are, it is quite cold; it is USDA winter hardiness zone 5, meaning an average winter low of

A dense, sculptural mound of *Arenaria tetraquetra*.

55

around -15° F, and the weather can be changeable and unpredictable. Sudden late frosts and early snowfalls are common. I visited in October, and when I awoke one morning to a blanket of snow, which then melted and turned into a warm and comfortable sunny day, none of the locals were concerned. When gardening here you really must choose plants that can take the wild swings of weather; it's not a good place for delicate plants that get frozen off by a late freeze. But, you know, these sorts of sudden weather changes are just what alpines and other plants for the rock garden are suited to—hence the profusion of such plants in Denver gardens.

Campanula topaliana coming into bloom against a rock.

Perhaps more important than the climate is the influence of Denver Botanic Gardens. Under the guidance of plant nerd and rock gardening visionaries like Panayoti Kelaidis and Mike Kintgen, it's a terrific example, testing ground, and learning site for local rock gardeners. It is spreading the gospel of growing rock garden and other locally adapted, water-wise plants in local gardens.

With the combination of influential local talent and an ideal climate for alpines, Denver has a predictable embarrassment of terrific rock gardens. I visited dozens of them and was blown away by lovely plants, beautiful stonework, sheets of lewisias, lush daphnes, fascinating collections of hardy cacti, and stunning hardy high-altitude South African succulents (all of which fail in my equally cold but much, much, wetter garden). How would I ever choose one to profile? Then we drove up to Helen's house.

I could almost see the influence of Helen's gardening prowess spreading up the street before we got to her house; as we got closer, the predictable suburban green lawns and shrubs started being broken up here and there by a cool alpine jewel. And then there was her house, with a small strip in front completely given over to a rock garden. She'd built up a mound of soil for drainage and to better display the plants, studded it with a few stones, and then planted it thickly with thriving alpine plants, from *Eriogonum,* with big heads of soft-pink flowers, to the tight, sculptural mounds of *Arenaria tetraquetra.*

It is a perfect little jewel box of a garden, meticulously maintained and richly planted. There are plenty of rocks and gravel mulch, but this isn't a garden of big open spaces and dramatically set off specimens; it's rather an intricate tapestry of different carpets and mounds and spikes growing and

interacting together. Though the plants are all well adapted to harsh, dry conditions, the effect is not spare or austere in the slightest; it is all warm and soft, with a heavy emphasis on silver leaves and pink flowers.

Helen is a very quiet, reserved woman, who, as I was madly snapping photos and gushing over the garden, kept quietly wondering why I thought it was anything worth taking pictures of. Far from being vain about her

Coping with changing weather

Wherever you garden, you'll have to deal with weather extremes and global climate change. We should all expect these extremes—be they hot or cold, wet or dry—to be more frequent and unpredictable. But even if the climate changes, you can keep gardening. It just means you need to think ahead and be ready to respond to weather vagaries as they come.

One looming challenge for many areas is drought, and most models predict that only to get worse. Even if you have plenty of water in your area now, consider turning back—or off—the irrigation in parts of your garden and exploring plants that will grow and thrive without added water. That way if a severe drought does set in, you'll have some beds that will thrive right through the worst of it, and you'll be familiar with good plant choices if you have to expand the low-water portions of your garden. Similarly, including tough plants adapted to colder and hotter conditions than you currently experience will have you prepared to come through that freak cold winter or hot summer with healthy, resilient plants in your garden.

Viewed toward the street, Helen's narrow front garden packs a ton of interest into a tiny space.

absolutely exquisite garden, she seems to be genuinely unaware of how incredibly striking it is.

But she clearly puts a lot of work into this beautiful garden. As we walked through, she pointed out a salvia, which, though lovely, she thought was a bit too large and loose for the space she had it in. It was going to have to come out—did we have any suggestions of what she could plant in its place? Looking at it, I had to say I could see what she meant; it didn't quite go with the rest of the garden. But it was so lovely! This is why I'll never be a really great gardener, I don't think—I don't have the focus and integrity of design to take out a plant that is okay and fine in order to replace it with a plant that is perfect and just right. But I came away with a commitment to learn the lesson of Helen's perfect little garden, and try to look at every plant I grow with a more critical eye. We'll see how far I get with that.

Phyllis Gustafson

MEDFORD, OREGON

It's all about the rocks

A spire of weathered driftwood behind tumbling *Eriogonum umbellatum* adds a sculptural note to one of the back crevice gardens.

I drove south from Portland to Medford, Oregon, to see Phyllis's garden; it's a drive of a few hours, but a world away in terms of climate in that dramatic way of things on the West Coast of the United States. Where I'm from you can drive for a couple hours and still be in essentially the same temperature and rainfall conditions, but out there, you pop around a mountain ▶

left › *Aethionema* 'Warley Rose' set by itself to shine.

center ›
Aethionema grandiflorum in full bloom.

right › White daisies of *Erigeron compositus* backed up by pink *Aethionema* 'Warley Rose'.

range or catch a different section of prevailing wind and everything changes. So while everything in Portland was wet and mossy, Medford was dry. Very dry. Wild calochortus was blooming on the grassy banks, and the hillsides were various shades of brown with small, scrubby oaks—and of course there were some truly amazing rock gardens.

The lack of rain, combined with reliable irrigation from mountain run-off, makes for golden rock gardening conditions. When you don't have to worry about anything getting too much water from excess rain and you can add water as you need it, you can fine-tune conditions to make just about anything happy. It is a little mind bending for someone like me who has always gardened in wetter climes. I don't irrigate anything planted in the ground. My attitude has always been that I water things in when they get planted, and after that either they survive or they don't. But for Phyllis, irrigation is a key aspect of the whole gardening operation. She emphasizes the

importance of—at least sometimes—running the irrigation during the day when you have time to walk around and make sure all the water is going where it is supposed to. She has stories of discovering why particular plants were failing when she eventually realized they weren't getting the water she thought they were.

Rock gardening is of course perfect for this climate, with western North America genera like *Penstemon* and *Eriogonum* absolutely thriving with far less water input than a more traditional garden or lawn. Medford has a richness of wonderful rock gardens to boast of, thanks mostly to two factors: Siskiyou Rare Plant Nursery and Josef Halda.

Siskiyou, though in recent years it has been sold to new owners and moved to a new location, was a pioneering rare plant—especially alpine or rock garden plant—nursery based in Medford. It's the source of many terrific varieties like the wonderful *Daphne* 'Lawrence Crocker',

and is to blame for many a rock gardener's passion in the western United States and elsewhere. Phyllis was a long-time employee and the main propagator at the nursery for years, and her expertise and many of her plants hail from there.

Josef Halda, the great Czech designer and gardener, has an old Medford connection and took many trips to the United States to design and build rock gardens for local enthusiasts. During those visits he often stayed with Phyllis and her husband, and he laid the stone for virtually all of the gardens on her property. He was an advocate of the crevice garden style, and laid out crevice gardens on a particularly grand scale—not neatly stacked layers of very thin, flat stones, but rather big, bold, dramatic rocks that make terrific homes for a wide range of plants and are fine art sculptures in their own right.

Phyllis's garden is richer for taking advantage of his expertise in both designing and laying the stones. Considering hiring an expert to lay the stony bones of your garden is often a good idea. For one, it saves you from destroying your back or knees trying to wrestle heavy rocks into place; it also ensures you get a framework that will be both aesthetically pleasing and physically stable without any unexpected settling and shifting over time.

Phyllis has taken that beautifully formed garden and used it as a canvas on which to paint with perfectly grown and arranged plants. Phyllis is a remarkable woman with a formidable set of skills and a profound knowledge of plants. Not only is she an expert on growing and propagating thanks to her time at Siskiyou Nursery, she's also a skilled botanist and coauthor of the field guide *Wildflowers of the Pacific Northwest*. On top of that deep technical knowledge, she's a talented artist; the walls of her house are full of her paintings. That artist's eye combined with intense technical knowledge of plants is pure gold when it comes to creating a garden.

Her artist's eye comes out in the garden in many ways. Little arrangements of beautifully combined colors, like dark sempervivums echoing the color of a dark-leaved geranium while contrasting perfectly with a silvery leaved sedum. Or the way she lets pulsatillas self-sow to produce graceful, natural looking drifts of lovely flowers, and later, the perhaps even more striking silky seed heads. Or letting individual plants shine—like an

clockwise from top › **A sunny, dry setting brings out the red tones in *Sedum rupestre* 'Angelina', echoed here perfectly by red sempervivums and a heuchera.**

A container of sempervivums sitting over *Geranium* 'Chocolate'.

The view from the street, with Phyllis's front door peeking around one of the massive front beds designed and built by Josef Halda.

***Delosperma nubigenum* blooming among the rocks.**

Hiring a designer

One of the smartest things you can do as a gardener is to know when you are out of your depth, and hire someone else to do what you can't or don't want to do yourself. If you are looking at a blank garden and don't know where to start putting in the background structure or where to place beds and big rocks, by all means consider hiring someone to come in and do that for you. Who you hire will depend on what you need done. Any good garden designer could help lay out beds and paths in a functional, pleasing way, and then it can be up to you to turn those beds into rock gardens. Or, if you are comfortable with the design process but don't have a good back, you may just need to hire some young, strong people to haul rocks and gravel into place while you direct them. A designer who specializes in rock gardens—though harder to find—will be able to take you from bare lawn to stone structures ready to plant. In all cases, it's best to get recommendations of people to hire from other local rock gardeners. Look at examples of their previous work, and spend some time talking with them to be sure you'll be able to work together. But if you can afford it and can find someone whose work you like, it is well worth the investment. Far easier to start off with a design you love than have to remove and rearrange everything a few years later when you realize it just isn't working.

absolutely perfectly grown *Aethionema* specimen completely covering itself in a solid sheet of clear-pink flowers sitting in a simple container by itself.

There are many lessons to be taken from Phyllis's garden. I came away committed to thinking long and hard about giving my garden great stony bones, and then using restraint in planting it up. Too often I want to mash everything in together. Using a painter's eye to make simple combinations, or letting single plants shine, is a lesson we can all take into our own gardens.

above › **Silky pulsatilla seed heads soften the edges of a gravel path between beds.**

below › **The front crevice garden.**

It's all about the plants

above › **Sensual undulations** of *Arenaria tetraquetra* **about to swallow up the rocks it was planted around.**

below › **Sedum in a trough is almost as beautiful in bud as it is in bloom.**

Kathy's garden is not far from Phyllis's, but despite being in the same neighborhood with the same climate and soil, the two gardens could hardly be more different. While Phyllis's garden is all massive stones arranged in dramatic patterns, Kathy's hardly has any stone at all. Her garden is a series of low berms built up with sand and gravel to provide good drainage for the ▶

plants. It is, in fact, a plant collection first and a garden second, her priority being to put plants where they will thrive, rather than where their colors will complement the surrounding plants or some other design consideration. Or at least that is what she told me. Whatever her method for planting, the resulting low tapestry of incredible plants is hard to argue with.

Among my favorite plants in her garden were the many specimens of *Asperula suberosa*, which forms beautiful undulating carpets of silvery foliage that transform in spring into sheets of baby-pink flowers. Rock-hard mats of *Arenaria tetraquetra* are another remarkable feature, and the many, many examples of *Eriogonum*—which hate my wet climate at home but here were looking lovely with their variously shaded fluffy heads of yellow and orange blooms. She grows stunning specimens of *Aquilegia scopulorum*,

left › **Blooming thyme and asperula make a warm combination.**

above › ***Primula sieboldii* blooming behind a trough of *Lewisia cotyledon* just getting started.**

top › **Kathy's low beds are packed with perfectly grown plants.**

Selling plants

If you, like Kathy, have a knack for propagation, the time may come when you find yourself looking at all the new plants you've created and wondering about making a profit from them. Having worked at a specialty nursery focusing on alpines, and seeing many similar excellent nurseries go out of business, I would say that we do desperately need more people producing and selling great alpine plants. However, most gardeners wildly underestimate how much work it is to make a business out of selling plants, especially specialty varieties for the rock garden. To feel your way into producing plants for sale, grow a few plants and let the local rock garden community know you'll be open for business on a certain day, or open your garden to a tour and have some plants for sale on the side. If you hate hearing people complain about the price or quality of your plants or worrying that the weather will wipe out all your profits, go back to growing for fun. If you find you love interacting with different people and making cool plants available, get a copy of Tony Avent's *So You Want to Start a Nursery?* and start making plans.

clockwise from top left › *Eriogonum* species with orange-red buds opening to soft yellow.

Nothing can beat the intense color of yellow linum blooming here in a trough.

Eriogonum species with soft yellow flowers and bright silver leaves.

one of the very best of the little alpine columbines, with tiny mounds of silvery blue leaves. But even better, I thought, were the various chance seedling columbines around the garden. Columbines are promiscuous to the extreme, and her various species had naturally hybridized to form some truly beautiful little specimens.

There were also some surprises, most notably huge stands of *Primula sieboldii* growing vigorously away in full sun. This is a plant I'd always grown in part shade, troubling to keep it from drying out. I was surprised to see it in the blazing southern Oregon sun, and clearly it was as happy as can be. Kathy told me that it simply goes dormant when it gets too hot in the summer, dying back to the roots and waiting out the heat and dry until it re-emerges (and flowers its head off) the next spring. Lesson learned—I'm moving some of mine out into the sun!

Part of the abundance of her garden may well stem from Kathy's side job running a small nursery at the garden, which is open seasonally to local rock gardeners. She grows everything from seed, a huge array of lovely little things in tiny little pots. A few, of course, came home with me; and I'm sure having all that nursery stock sitting around means she puts far more things into her garden than the average gardener could afford. Another plug for learning to propagate your own plants, so you can plant up a garden on the scale that Kathy has.

left › *Primula
sieboldii* thriving
in full sun before
going dormant
for the summer.

below left ›
*Asperula
suberosa* coming
into flower.

right › **A chance** *Aquilegia* **hybrid that seeded itself in; may we all be so lucky to have weeds like this!**

below › *Delosperma* 'Red Mountain' in full bloom.

Stella Rankin

MIDLOTHIAN, SCOTLAND

Pathways of a designer

Smooth lawn
suddenly gives
way to a hillside
rock garden.

When I visited Stella's garden, I drove up
the narrow lane to their simple, modern
house, went through the gate, and caught
my breath. What appears to be an ordinary
garden a mere 20-minute drive from
Edinburgh is revealed as perched on the
edge of a nearly vertical drop, giving lovely
views of the Scottish countryside. Once
you look down from the view, you find the ▶

hillside itself crisscrossed with gentle paths leading you down through a treasure trove of even more plants.

clockwise from top left › **A saxifrage nestled between a rock and hard place, ready to bloom.**

Primula marginata **thriving in the crack of a rock.**

Blue *Lithodora diffusa* **backed by a mass of beautiful** *Erica.*

Stella is the owner of Kevock Garden Plants, producing lovely alpine plants at her wholesale nursery. She also designs gardens for others—her garden shows off both her design chops and her taste for exquisite plants. Her garden displays a wide range of plants, from the perhaps less unusual but still lovely sempervivums and *Sedum spathulifolium* 'Cape Blanco', with powdery white new growth that contrasts strongly with the red tones of older leaves below, along with exquisite specimens like *Lewisia tweedyi* putting up surreally large flowers subtly shaded in warm tones of yellow fading into rose and salmon over the basal rosette of succulent leaves. And one of my favorite plants, easy to grow but rarely cultivated, *Polygala chamaebuxus*, forming a shrublet with glossy evergreen leaves studded with fragrant flowers that improbably combine bright yellow and bright pink, which ought to clash but look terrific instead.

I love that in this garden, the rock garden isn't kept tucked away in one section. As you move down the slope, you pass stone walls with alpines between rhododendrons, a shady section with trilliums in bloom, then another bed of alpines. Sometimes rock gardeners give in to the plant collector impulse, and the beds feel less like a garden and more like a formal catalog of plants. Nothing could be further from the case here, where the

Lewisia tweedyi blooming in a container.

beds are beautifully designed with colors complementing each other and packed with little vignettes where magnolias bloom with a striking background of black mondo grass, or blue lithodora shines against the backdrop of purple heather.

In addition to the perfect plant combinations, I have squirreled away in my mind several design features of this

above › **Neatly built stone walls create terraces of planting space.**

right › **View from the top of the garden looking out on the Scottish hills.**

above left › **One of the many paths leading you gently up and down the slope to appreciate each planting.**

above right › **Looking up the hillside to Stella's beautiful modern home.**

left › **The hillside garden seen from below, crisscrossed by many paths for close inspection.**

Polygala chamaebuxus with evergreen leaves and its unique, colorful flowers creeping between rocks.

garden to try and recreate in my own garden. First, with alpine beds sprin-kled among larger trees and shrubs, you see the garden a bit at a time as dif-ferent plants come into view, rather than all in one big sweep. The feeling is intimate and exciting, and makes the garden seem much, much larger than it truly is, slowly unfolding as you explore it.

The other design aspect—which also works to make the garden seem much larger than it is—is the placement and number of paths leading you through the garden as you go up and down the hillside. When gardening on a steep slope, building a smooth, stable, navigable path is a lot of work, and so I think people often skimp. But Stella hasn't, with many paths moving along the length of the hill, some only going a little ways up or down, with the result that you get to see each bed from multiple angles. Many walls and beds first seen from above give you one distinct view, and then later you come up to it from below, so the tiny alpines are now seen nearly at eye level. The two views are so different—one showing the broad forms and col-ors of the plants, the other showing off their fine details up close—that you get two distinctively different aesthetic effects from each small bed.

Coloring with confidence

Many rock gardeners are more collectors than designers; their gardens are full of perfectly grown unusual plants arranged with no particular plan other than positioning each plant where it will grow the best. Beautiful plants will always make for a beautiful garden, but there is no reason not to bring sharp design sensibilities to the rock garden. Pick a color scheme, and select plants with the flowers and foliage that will match it. You can dream up a set of colors (yellow, purples, and blues, say, or hot red, orange, and yellow) or you can borrow one from anywhere—a friend once designed a garden based on the colors in a loved piece of vintage fabric. You could start with the colors seen in a flower arrangement, or use a palette generator like coolors.co. In every garden, one dominant color will be that of foliage, but in the rock garden, remember that the color of your rocks and gravel mulch will be a dominant design element as well. Don't be above taking a bit of stone or a piece of a favorite plant with you to a nursery so you can see how different plants will look with them.

This all-white rock garden is a picture of elegance.

Michael Riley

NEW YORK, NEW YORK

If you can garden here, you can garden anywhere

A few years ago I attended a North American Rock Garden Society (NARGS) winter study weekend in Pittsburgh, Pennsylvania. They were having a trough competition. There were a lot of lovely planted troughs of various styles and types, but one of them really stood out: simple, beautifully planted, not full of ▶

A peat block container with moss, shortia, ferns, and *Rhododendron campylogynum.*

flashy flowers, but perfectly grown and arranged plants. It was far and away my favorite—and the judges agreed, awarding it first place. I was so impressed by the trough that I wanted to know more about who had planted it, so I met (briefly, at this point) Michael Riley, a soft-spoken, white-haired gentleman who lives and gardens—on a rooftop in Manhattan.

Yes, that's right, Manhattan in New York City. I was very intrigued. I certainly wasn't thinking that I would find a terrific rock garden smack dab in the middle of one of the largest, busiest cities in the world. When I found myself in New York later for an event at the New York Botanical Garden, I sent Michael a message asking if I could come by, and he very kindly said I could. I have to say: I rarely visit great private gardens by taking the subway, getting off by Central Park, and then walking a couple blocks through tall apartment buildings.

I knew I had gotten to the right building when I walked up and noticed I was seeing a lot of green through the windows of one floor. Sure sign that a gardener lives there! I rang the bell, came up the stairs, and when Michael opened the front door, the glimpse of green I'd seen from the street didn't begin to prepare me for what I saw as I walked in. Michael has taken an entire wall of his spacious apartment, covered it with a layer of cork, installed a misting system, and planted the whole thing with orchids, bromeliads, and other plants that normally make a living perched on the branches of trees in tropical forests. It is a stunning show, and just a hint of what a talented gardener Michael is. I couldn't wait to get up to the roof and see his troughs.

When I was talking to Michael about coming to visit, he kept telling me that his rooftop was not a garden, rather just a collection of troughs and containers arranged to grow the plants the best, not necessarily to look the best together. Seeing it myself, I can see what he means, to a point: it is a utilitarian space. But rather than not call it a garden, I would call it a collection of gardens, as each container is an exquisitely arranged and designed tiny little garden, each one different and beautiful.

Michael's other garden: his apartment wall covered with tropical plants.

A Manhattan rooftop is a harsh environment: blustery wind, bright sun, and the potential for sudden swings from hot to cold. It is, I suppose, a bit like a mountaintop in those ways, so it is little surprise that alpine plants are a great choice for these conditions. Not to mention that their small size allows him to make the most of a very limited space.

Michael has learned how to make the very best growing environment for his plants. Frequent watering is his number one tip, followed by stretching a shade cloth over most of his plants in the summer to give a little shelter from the sun and wind. Choosing the right things to fill his containers with is another key aspect to growing well in these conditions. For most of his alpines he uses sand, which has great drainage but still holds enough water. And in his containers he also swears by not just putting rocks on the surface as decoration, but also placing long rocks all the way down to the bottom of the container before filling it with the sand and plants. He feels the deeply plunged rocks help guide the roots of the plants

Finding a place to garden

Not everyone in an urban area has access to a rooftop like Michael's, but even if you live in an apartment without a balcony or patio, you can still find a place to have a rock garden. The ever-growing popularity of allotment and community gardens in cities around the world has made it easier than ever to get your hands on a bit of ground. Just check to be sure that these often vegetable-centric spaces are okay with you putting in a rock garden instead of the usual tomatoes and sunflowers. But even if they aren't, don't give up. Between 2003 and 2015, I moved a lot and gardened in six different spaces, only one of which I owned—all the others were places that people let me use. Your gardening friends are your first resource, often in unexpected ways: one of my first garden spaces I tracked down because a friend's brother's friends' friend had space in her yard that she was willing to let me use. More recently, a post on social media netted me no fewer than three different offers for additional space to create gardens in. I've also had success putting ads requesting land on craigslist, the online classifieds site, and contacting my city to get permission to use a vacant lot near where I was living at the time. So there is no excuse—wherever you are, you can find a place to have a rock garden!

These violas growing in a community vegetable plot are evidence that you can have a rock garden in an unlikely place.

to grow deeply along the surface of the rock, preventing them from growing shallow root systems that are more prone to drying out.

But some of his containers are totally different. In addition to troughs filled with sand, he has solid blocks of peat resting in shallow plastic trays. The story is that a friend of his saw a truck at a gas station loaded with blocks of peat freshly cut from a bog on their way to being ground up to make potting soil, and she managed to buy a carload of the peat blocks. Michael got some of the blocks from her, and the rest is history. The blocks make amazing growing spaces for delicate woodland treasures that want moist, acidic soil. Miniature rhododendrons, really exquisite (and notoriously difficult) shortias, lovely little thalictrums, and of course, very happy colonies of mosses. They form tiny slices of a moist, shady woodland in the middle of an exposed city rooftop.

Recently planted troughs, one with flat stones to create a miniature crevice garden.

Gardening on a rooftop has its own set of unique challenges. No need to worry about rabbits or deer; yet some of his containers are surrounded by chicken wire cages to keep out pigeons of all things, which have a voracious taste for the leaves of some of his more treasured plants. Then there was the time that the people who rent the apartment directly below his rooftop complained that their door wasn't closing right anymore—and Michael realized that the door was directly below his biggest mass of heavy, wet, sand-filled troughs. That required a little rearrangement of containers to redistribute the weight a bit more evenly to stop the roof from sagging so the door could close flush again.

So every garden site, no matter how unusual, has its challenges and opportunities. But if you ever find yourself thinking you would like to have a garden but just don't have the space, I believe that Michael has proven you wrong. You can garden—and garden well—anywhere.

Growing for show

The surreal flowers of *Physoplexis comosa* are truly one of a kind.

I first got to know Cliff through Facebook. If you didn't already know, there is a bewilderingly wonderful array of plant-centric groups on Facebook, and Cliff is a constant presence on some of the rock gardening groups' posts. He posts frequently with beautiful images of perfectly grown plants; some are from other gardens or his trips to see alpine ▶

plants in the wild, but often from his own garden near Manchester. When I set out to write this book and was coming up with a list of gardens to possibly profile, Cliff's name was at the top of the list, so I sent him a message. He replied quickly, saying he thought I'd be disappointed if I came to the garden as it is only 15 ft. × 30 ft. I was stunned. Given the sheer diversity and range of plants I had seen pictures of, I had imagined the garden would be much, much larger. But if anything that made me want to include his garden in this book even more, because it perfectly illustrates the fact that rock gardening is the best option for people with very limited room to garden. If Cliff loved roses or big perennials, he'd be very limited in what he could grow. But a mere 15 ft. × 30 ft. garden is enough to grow huge numbers of fascinating alpine plants.

Cliff's front garden is full of raised beds and troughs showcasing classic alpines like primulas, pulsatillas, and the perfectly fringed purple bells of soldanella. He also has some really wonderful saxifrages; a trough full of them shows to perfection their dense mounds giving way to solid domes of flowers in pink, white, and yellow.

Cliff's back garden shows his true love as a rock gardener, where his focus is less on how the plants look in his garden than on how they'll look on a show bench. Alpine plant shows are few and far between in the United States but alive and well in the United Kingdom. Gardeners like Cliff work to grow plants in pots to insane peaks of perfection so they can be transported in full bloom to the show bench where they will be judged and compared, and hopefully will win awards. Growing for show is an entirely different sort of gardening, where one is focused on getting a plant to look absolutely perfect for just that moment in time when the judging is happening, rather than (as I do) merely hoping that a plant grows and looks good. In addition to the fascinating technical challenge of growing this way, it is a magnificent approach to focus in on and enjoy the beauty and detail of individual specimens on their own, rather than having them get lost in the hustle and bustle of the main garden.

left › **The troughs and beds of Cliff's front garden seen from above.**

below › **A trough of saxifrages coming into bloom.**

And then there is the social aspect—gardening can be a bit of a loner's activity. But getting the chance to take your plants to a show and display them for a bunch of other plant-obsessed people is a nice change from the regular solitary weeding and planting.

Cliff grows many choice specimens, and placing them singly in a pot really draws the eye in to focus on every detail of the plant. A specimen

Growing for show

Gardening can be a solitary hobby. Shows are a solution to that, allowing you to interact with other passionate growers while showing off the plants you are most proud of, and admiring what others have brought. If you want to start showing your plants, the first step is to visit shows in your area, talk to the judges, and look at the other entries so you can get a sense of the competition and what the judges are looking for. If there are no shows in your area (as is sadly the case in much of North America), talk to your local rock garden society about starting one. Once you've been to a show or set a date to start a new one, go back to your garden and see what is looking particularly stunning in the garden. Timing is critical here. An absolutely perfect dianthus that peaked two weeks before the show will win you no ribbons. You can tweak the timing a little, keeping them warm to hurry or cool to slow them down, but your best bet is not to put all your eggs in one basket and groom early and late plants for the show so that whatever the weather does, you'll have something ready.

This beautifully grown specimen of *Saxifraga* 'Jenkinsiae' shows what can be achieved by growing a choice alpine in a pot.

Pulsatilla and primroses greet spring in one of the front troughs.

of *Ranunculus parnassifolius* 'Nuria' is beautiful, and all the more so once you take a moment to look closely and see the way the dark-red hues of the stems and petioles set off the delicate pink-veined flowers.

The number one plant in his garden that I wish I could grow well is *Physoplexis comosa*, with totally unique clusters of flowers, each one lavender at the base and stretching into a long, narrow spire of almost black. Cliff insists it isn't that difficult to grow, at least in his climate: he simply gives them very lean, well-drained conditions with lots of limestone grit and chunks of tufa and limestone mixed into the potting medium, and a few pieces of tufa placed just under the crown of the plant to keep it from getting soggy. The plants thrive year-round outside in his garden, with no fuss or added fertilizer, and bloom their heads off. I might just be inspired to try it again. And I'm going to have to grow more alpines in pots. Even if I don't bring them to a show, it would be fun to be able to bring a perfect specimen out as a table centerpiece or display it in a prime spot on the patio while in full glory.

Techniques

Growing rock garden plants isn't difficult, but knowing their needs will start you off in the right direction.

Evolving on the tops of mountains or on the harsh, dry steppe gives rock garden plants unique forms and aesthetic appeal as ▶

well as significantly different needs in the garden than the larger, lusher, lowland perennials and annuals most gardeners are familiar with. So if you are already a gardener, becoming a rock gardener involves a little change of focus and rethinking some assumptions. In the world of rock gardening, you won't be hearing that constant refrain of "fertile, well-drained, evenly moist soil" that we've all heard recommended time and time and time again. Rock gardeners eschew the moist and the fertile, preferring lean, gritty soil as the perfect home for their alpine treasures. Not only is the ideal soil different, but creating a rock garden bed is quite unlike laying out a new perennial border as well. Rock gardens are typically more three-dimensional affairs, constructed and built rather than simply dug and amended, with mulches of gravel rather than shredded bark and plants growing in rock crevices rather than double-dug borders.

Though creating a rock garden is different than making other sorts of gardens, the techniques and methods involved aren't difficult; in this section we'll go over everything you need to know. We'll look at the various styles of rock gardens, explore their different aesthetics and how the type of garden influences how plants will grow, and delve into the mechanics of constructing rock gardens. When the bones of your garden structure are in place, we'll talk about the soil for the rock garden, discussing the types of mixes that make for the happiest plants, the ingredients and amendments you can use, and how plants will respond to the different conditions you create. If you have limited space or want to highlight a particularly special, tiny plant, container gardens are the answer, so we'll explore the details of gardening in containers—how to choose the right container, plants to grow in them, and how to keep those plants happy in their small quarters.

The biggest factor in making sure your rock garden thrives is to understand your local climate, so we'll delve deep into all the variables from heat to cold to rain or the lack thereof, and how those influence your garden. We'll talk about how to work with your climate to find plants that will thrive with minimal care, and how to push against your conditions to grow a wider range of plants. Finally, we'll discuss how to track down the best plants for your new rock garden, as well as explain techniques like starting plants from seed and rooting cuttings that will allow you to get some of the coolest, most unusual plants without breaking the budget. In short, this section is about giving you know-how, a solid foundation of information and techniques to get you rock gardening successfully and with confidence.

Styles and Construction

In a practical sense, all a rock garden needs to do is provide a good home for your plants and look attractive to you, the gardener. There are many different ways of achieving this. As we walk through some of them, don't think of these as firm definitions or recipes to follow, but as ideas and jumping off points to get you thinking about how you want to structure your rock garden and make good homes for the plants you want to grow.

There is great potential to explore new forms and approaches to designing rock gardens. For example, the traditional rock garden styles, with few exceptions, are staunchly informal and naturalistic—aiming to imitate, in miniature, the landscape of a

Most people expect rock gardens to be naturalistic and informal, but why shouldn't they be daring and modern?

mountaintop or stony ridge. These approaches are beautiful (and strongly to my personal taste), but there is no reason that you can't take these ideas and go off in different directions, exploring more geometric and formal designs. You'll see I also talk about railroad and fairy gardens, two garden styles that are certainly not included in traditional rock gardening. While the purists may object, a fairy garden is, to my mind, simply rock gardening with props. The basic principles of using small plants to create miniature landscapes are the same whether you are building a rock garden or a fairy garden; the traditional rock gardener uses naturalistic ornamentation in the form of stones, while the railroad and fairy gardeners use more man-made forms.

And there is potential for rock gardening styles to continue to expand through experimentation and cross-pollination with other styles. I've never seen a Victorian-style knot garden made of alpines, but you absolutely could create one, or borrow from other miniature landscape traditions like bonsai and penjing. The options are endless, and when designing your garden always remember that the person whose opinion matters is yours, the person who is going to be living and working in the garden you create. Make your garden your own, and expert opinions be damned.

ROCKERY

When I use the word *rockery*, I'm thinking of the classic rock garden, a mound of soil (or sand or gravel or whatever medium you decide to grow in) often supported around the edges with larger rock to form an informal raised bed, with more rock scattered around in an aesthetically pleasing manner. There are many shades of this general approach—from the older, unabashedly fantastic and artificial constructions of the Edwardian period, with rocks piled and cemented together in great wild mountains, to the more strictly naturalistic approaches championed by rock gardening god Reginald Farrer. Flip through the gardens profiled in this book and see what appeals most to you, then keep in mind some guidelines that will help you arrange your rocks in an aesthetically pleasing way.

If you are going for a naturalistic approach, think about geology, and arrange stones in lines to form ridges and strata of rock rather than

Over-the-top exuberance of rock at the Aysgarth Edwardian Rock Garden.

A rich carpet of alpine plants at Ambleside Road in Surrey.

scattering them here and there randomly. One excellent approach for any informal design is to use odd numbers. You've probably heard this before in terms of using plants in threes and fives. Rocks are the same. Placing them in clusters of odd numbers will look more natural and less contrived than single rocks scattered here and there or in pairs. If you live in an area where there is exposed natural rock, you will almost certainly want to match the rock in your garden to that of the surrounding area. No matter how carefully you arrange them, a garden made of limestone slabs will never look particularly natural if there are sandstone bluffs all around you.

If you are aiming for a less natural or more formal look, the options are endless, but perhaps the most important thing to keep in mind is to commit fully to your look. An informal, curving bed is lovely, as is a strictly formal straight line. But nothing looks worse than a line that was intended to be straight but actually is just slightly crooked. To modify the old saying about carpentry: measure twice, move rocks once.

In all cases, it is generally wise to limit yourself to one type of rock in a bed. I have seen beds done beautifully using a mix of different stones, but usually they end up looking like a jumbled mess. Keeping to just one type of stone in the bed is easy and always looks great.

Before you buy a load of huge, beautiful rocks, be sure you have a plan to move them into position. Small stones can be moved simply by brute force, but for larger rock you will want the proper tools to make the task easier and less likely to result in a damaged back. A simple hand truck will make moving moderately sized rocks a great deal easier, and laying down a sheet of plywood over the path will make a smooth surface for the wheels and minimize soil compaction. For larger rocks, consider either renting proper power equipment or hiring a team to move the rocks into place. A little investment in people with the correct tools and know-how will make your life easier and save you possible injury.

One final thought: newly placed rocks almost always look a little artificial and will look increasingly natural and at home once they've settled into the soil and are nestled in between growing plants. It is worth fussing around with your rocks to get them in an arrangement you like, but don't stress about it too much. Rocks are always beautiful.

SCREES AND MORAINES

Scree is a technical geological term, referring to a place where erosion or a landslide has resulted in coarse rocks and gravel mounded at the base

Ev Whittemore's scree-style garden in North Carolina.

of a slope. Natural scree will therefore be a mound of different sizes of rocks, gravel, and possibly some soil as well, mixed together irregularly. A moraine is a similar formation, but created by a melting glacier. In the rock gardening world, scree usually means a bed made of larger rocks and gravel rather than soil or sand. A rock gardener's moraine is a similar bed, but with the addition of water flowing under the rocks to give the plants the ability to get their roots down to constantly fresh, cool water. Moraines are clearly a bit elaborate to build, as you need to make an artificial stream (unless by some chance you have a natural brook in your garden) and then build the bed on top of it. Screes, in contrast, can be among the easiest rock gardens to build—as easy as ordering a truckload of cheap fill gravel and directing the truck slowly forward as it dumps out the gravel. The result is a long bed of coarse gravel; add a few larger rocks where they look like they'd be pleasing, and plant. Because the coarse materials of a scree are so well drained, they're usually not well suited to very dry climates. But in rainy areas, where your primary concern is keeping plants from getting too wet, they work beautifully. Scree beds are also a good option if you don't have easy access to big rocks, or don't know enough young people with strong backs to move them—they can be lovely without any large stones at all. A

A patch of scree blends smoothly with perennial borders, but grows alpines beautifully thanks to a layer of gravel.

variation on this is simply piling a layer of sand and gravel over your regular soil, in the regular garden. Even just a few inches will be enough to make a lot of nice alpines happy, and it's a way to blend them visually into perennial beds or other parts of the garden.

ROCK WALLS

Old, dry-laid stone walls will often, over time, become home to various small plants in the cracks and crevices. But if you build a wall specifically to house plants, you'll be able to grow a far greater diversity. Planted walls can be beautiful, and they provide a unique design effect. Putting plants up in a stone wall is a lovely way to display the tiniest forms where they can be appreciated; of course creeping and trailing plants never look better than where they have room to grow at length. Walls, being vertical, also provide exceptional drainage, making them a great place to grow particularly wet-sensitive plants. Growing on walls is also uniquely wonderful for plants like lewisias that can rot not only due to excess water at their roots, but also because rainwater can lodge in the rosettes of the leaves. Planting them on a wall turns that rosette sideways so it doesn't hold water, allowing them to thrive in climates that would otherwise be too rainy.

The traditional rock garden planted wall is made of stone with a mass of soil behind it, either as a retaining wall or a freestanding wall with soil between the two sides of stone. Plants are inserted as the wall is built (usually), or tucked in afterward into pockets of soil between the rocks, allowing them to send roots back through the wall into the cool, moister interior. One strategy for making pockets for planting is to take old socks, fill them with soil, and then tuck them in between the rocks as the wall is built. One final key feature of a wall that will be a good habitat for plants is to lay the stones so that they slope down toward the inside of the wall, so that when rain falls it is directed into the soil rather than draining away.

An exciting and beautiful variant on the traditional planted wall is a tufa wall. Tufa is a lightweight, highly porous limestone rock. Unlike a typical wall where plants must grow in the spaces between the rocks, tufa is porous enough so that some plants can grow directly on the tufa itself—very drought-tolerant species like some sedums and sempervivums will thrive

above › **This dry wall explodes with color from helianthemums, campanulas, hardy geraniums, and corydalis.**

left › **A tufa wall at the Royal Botanic Garden Edinburgh grows a wide range of choice alpines in holes drilled into the rock.**

this way. Planting pockets for other plants can be created by drilling holes into the soft rock and tucking the plants right into the hole. In most climates, a drip irrigation line at the top of the wall will be necessary to ensure adequate moisture, particularly as the plants are getting established.

It is important not to confuse the planted rock wall with green walls, which are quite a different thing. Green walls typically are small containers or frames of soil mounted on an existing wall, and often heavily irrigated so that water-loving plants can be grown on them. Rock garden plants can be grown on those types of green walls as well, with the added bonus of needing less irrigation than what is usually used on a green wall. One comment: green walls typically are designed to be completely covered by vegetation, while with a planted stone wall the plants are used more as an accent to complement the beauty of the stone itself. So the best choices for a planted stone wall will be small, tight plants that won't obscure the stonework, like the dense mounds of *Gypsophila aretioides*, while more rapidly spreading plants, such as vigorous *Delosperma*, would be a better choice to get the sheet-of-green effect of a typical green wall.

CREVICE

Crevice gardens were popularized by Czech rock gardeners and have spread widely among rock gardeners elsewhere in the world. The inspiration in nature for a crevice garden is exposed, cracked strata of rock, but to be honest, the built version often doesn't look (at least to me) much like anything you're likely to find in nature. Crevice gardens do, however, look extremely cool. Basically, you take a lot of flat stones and place them vertically (or more typically, at a slight angle) with thin strips of soil between them. In addition to having kick-ass aesthetics, crevice gardens have some practical advantages in the way they grow plants. Every gardener I've talked to agrees that plants grow smaller and tighter in the crevice garden, and a wider range of plants will grow than in a traditional rock garden. I expect a large part of the miniaturizing effect is due to the plants growing in a limited amount of soil. Like the regular root pruning and small containers of bonsai that miniaturize trees, the narrow crevice of soil restricts root growth to keep plants smaller. However, unlike growing in a container where roots can circle and become pot-bound, the wide and deep crevice means roots can keep growing out and down, despite the restrictions of the narrow crevice. Another possible reason for the crevice garden effect is that since the narrow opening forces roots to grow down more than out, crevice plants are deep-rooted and better able to cope with drought. Whatever the reason, crevice gardens are beautiful and excellent for growing the choicest, most difficult of plants.

The width of the crevices makes a big difference in a crevice garden, both visually and in how plants grow. Smaller crevices obviously require smaller plants and tend to look more naturalistic—as if the garden were one stone that developed fine cracks. Larger crevices will act more like a typical rockery and allow larger plants to be grown. You can of course vary the width of the crevices within the same garden, with larger and smaller cracks to support a whole range of different-sized plants.

A wide variety of stone can be used in a crevice garden. An ideal choice would be a stone like slate or a strong limestone that can either be split or cut into thin, narrow slabs without worrying about them cracking. Stones intended to be used as paving are often ideal. The individual slabs can be thin or thick depending on your aesthetic preference; thinner stones

above › **A crevice garden built by Kenton Seth in Denver, Colorado, with narrow spaces for the smallest of plants.**

below › **A new crevice garden under construction by Kenton Seth for a client in Denver, Colorado.**

generally will be best for small crevices, while the thickest will be more suitable for large-scale installations.

When building a crevice garden, you'll want to keep a couple of things in mind. First, you want to make sure that all the crevices run at the same angle—it really does look better that way. Double-check each stone when you place it to make sure the angle matches those of the other stones. Small variations are fine and will be covered somewhat once you get the garden planted. Second, take care with the stones at the edges of the garden. A large crevice garden is essentially a raised bed, and the stones on the edges need to be able to support the weight of the soil and other stones inside. Bury those outside stones deeply in the soil base, to perhaps half their length, and pack your soil in around them tightly to make sure they form a strong foundation for the garden.

If you don't have access to the large, flat stones required to build a crevice garden, or don't want to deal with hauling big, heavy stones into place, casting hypertufa faux stones is a good alternative; they are much lighter in weight, and you can cast them in just the sizes you want.

Once your stones are in place, fill in the crevices with the sand or soil mixture for your plants to grow in. The smaller the crevices, the harder it will be to work the soil down into them completely, and there will almost certainly be some settling down over time. Save some soil mix for the first couple of months so you can replace any soil that settles down deeper. Rain (or heavy irrigation) can also easily wash the soil mix out from between the crevices of a newly built crevice garden. Once the plants have settled in, their roots will hold the soil. In the meantime, wedging small chips of stone at regular intervals between the crevices, especially at the edges of the garden, will hold it in place.

MINIATURE LANDSCAPES: RAILROAD AND FAIRY GARDENS

I always say that railroad gardens and fairy gardens are just rock gardens with props. For some, the props—be they model train stations or cute fairy figurines—are the whole focus. But many other gardens are a wonderful marriage of diminutive plant forms and tiny buildings to create

Miniature gardens are really just a specialized form of a rock garden.

miniaturized landscapes that are a fascinating and different take on the typical rock garden scaled-down, idealized mountaintop. Given the blatant artificiality of fairy gardening décor, they're probably not the best choice for strictly naturalistic design. Indulge your whimsy and build something fantastic for your fairies.

CHOOSING AND PREPARING THE SITE

As you are thinking through the different styles and approaches, there are a few important practical considerations to keep in mind as you design your new rock garden.

First, a good rock garden needs to provide good habitat for plants to grow. With the exception of highly porous rocks like tufa, plants don't grow on rocks themselves, but in bits of soil and sand between the stones. So when designing a garden or placing stone, always think about the spaces you are leaving for growing things, whether a broad expanse of open sandy soil or a narrow crevice between two stones. And if you are fortunate to have a garden with lots of natural stone, your task will often be creating spaces for the plants to grow in, either by removing stone to create openings or by adding stones to build up planting pockets behind them.

You also want to be sure you are going to be very happy with where you've placed your new stones, so use garden hose, turf paint, or some other temporary marker to line out the dimensions of the bed and then live with it for a few days. Make sure it isn't blocking the easiest way to walk from the house to the garage, or the path your dogs like to take when chasing a ball. Go inside and see how easily you can see the new bed through your windows. Kneel at the edge of the potential bed and see if you can reach into the center to pull a weed. If you can't reach, plan on a small path or stepping-stones for access. If you have trouble visualizing a new bed, try this: take some pictures of your space, print them out, and lay out drawings of potential designs or cutout flower images from catalogs on top of the photo to help you see what the new bed will look like. Ask gardening friends with taste you respect to give advice and comments. Anything you can do to get a good idea of what your new bed will look like before you start construction will help you make good design choices that you won't wind up wanting to change after it is finished.

Once you know what you are building, take the time to eliminate weeds. Starting with a fresh, weed-free space will make maintaining the new bed easier by several orders of magnitude, especially if you are starting with rough turf or wild areas, or the ground is contaminated with vicious perennial weeds like ground elder or bindweed. There are several ways to do this. Smothering weeds with thick layers of newspaper, cardboard, or even black plastic works well. Herbicides are also a possibility. Tilling the soil does kill weeds, but I don't like it; it fluffs up the soil, which will then slowly sink and dislodge your rocks over time. Tilling also stirs up dormant weed seeds, which can sit a long time underground before germinating when brought to the surface. Brigitta Stewart, my former boss at Arrowhead Alpines, always says that you should do weed control for a full year before planting a new bed; that way you can be absolutely sure you've gotten everything killed and there are no seeds waiting to germinate. That isn't always possible, but when you do have the time it is a great idea and will save a lot of work down the road.

When planning new beds, remember to start small. You can always expand, and a new garden is always *much* more work than an established one—there will be a flush of weeds attempting to move into the newly disturbed, mostly open space. You'll always try a few things that for some reason refuse to grow and have to be replaced, and you generally have to learn the rhythm of what the plants need and when. By all means plan out many, many beds all at once, but install them a little bit at a time so you aren't overwhelmed with the maintenance of too many new spaces—not to mention the strain on the pocketbook of trying to plant them all at one go. One of the great joys of gardening is the eternal process of building and expanding and trying new things. Don't blow that all at once. Leave some of your garden for your future self—who, by the way, will be more experienced and confident than you are now—to design and plant.

Finally, don't be afraid to call in a professional. Once heavy stones are in place you are pretty much stuck with them, so it is worth investing in an expert eye to make sure the bones of your garden are going to look good. And even if you are confident in your ability to design your new garden, you might want to hire someone with a strong back to do the actual moving of rocks and gravel. Hiring a few local teenagers for a couple of afternoons is almost certain to be cheaper than back surgery because you did something stupid.

That is my mini tour of some of the main styles and approaches to building a rock garden. Start with your own ideas, combine them with the images and inspiration contained in the garden profiles in this book, and you'll have lots of options to choose from in designing your garden bed. Do things on a small scale first, take some time to see what is working and what isn't, and go from there.

Soil

If you are already a gardener, particularly if you are used to growing vegetables, forget everything you think you know about soil. Soil for rock gardens is a special case, and the perfect rock garden soil is quite different from the perfect soil for a vegetable or perennial garden. You need to remember that most of the plants you are growing in a rock garden are native to mountaintops, evolved to eke out a happy life with very little in the way of what we usually think of as soil, and a lot more rocks and gravel. That is what they're adapted to, and that is the sort of soil where they usually grow best. It may seem that despite their rough-and-ready adaptations, these plants would respond to more prosperous digs with happiness, but it doesn't really work that way, at least not usually. First, that coarse, rocky soil with limited organic matter that doesn't hold water is a very inhospitable place for the various pathogens that cause root and crown rots. Usually living relatively free of these pathogens, many alpine and dryland plants succumb quickly when placed in wetter conditions where these pathogens can thrive.

Second, it is worth remembering that a lot of what we do to normal garden soil is making it rich and fertile so that we can, in the words of a fertilizer ad, "grow plants twice as big." Twice as big isn't exactly a good thing to rock gardeners. The appeal of a lot of these plants is their tight growth habit: dense, sculptural buns, mounds, and mats. Too much fertility will usually result in lush, loose growth that rather spoils the point.

Of course there are exceptions to all of these rules. Though most of the plants we grow in a rock garden come from thin, rocky soils, there certainly are wonderful plants for rock gardens that come from rich soils that are high in organic matter. This is particularly true of miniature plants for shady rock gardens, such as asarums, shortias, and a few other specific groups. These are the exceptions, however, rather than the rule, and your default for rock gardening soil should thin, rocky, and lean.

In general, the perfect place for most alpine plants to grow in would be a mass of soil raised up above the surrounding area, mostly made of a quick-draining material like coarse sand or grit, with a layer of gravel mulch at the top, and potentially a fine-textured, wetter material (be it sand or even clay) at the bottom. Why is that such a great place to grow alpines? Well, let's walk through some of the factors at work in detail.

DRAINAGE

Drainage is the most important factor in creating good soil for a rock garden. Whatever soil you use, it needs to allow water to drain quickly and easily so the plant does not stay waterlogged. Most critically, water needs to be able to move quickly away from the crown of the plant. Most pathogens that cause alpine plants to rot out don't attack the roots themselves, but rather the base of the plant right where it meets the soil; so ensuring that water can drain away from the top inch or two of the soil very rapidly is of utmost importance. The tight growth habit of most rock garden plants slows the normal drying of the crown of the plant, making drainage at the soil surface even more critical. There are three main factors that influence how well a soil mix will drain: pore size, soil depth, and siting.

Pores in soil are the openings, the spaces between the particles of actual soil. When thinking about soil, we often talk about the things that it is made of—sand, clay, organic matter, and so on—but the most important part of soil is the space in between. This is where roots grow and where they get the water and air they need. Big, coarse particles like gravel or grit leave many large openings between them. As the particles get smaller, from sand to silt to the smallest, clay, the pores get smaller as well. Smaller pores hold water better while larger pores let it drain away. We all know this from experience. Water poured onto a pile of marbles will quickly run out, while a sponge or paper towel—made up of lots and lots of tiny pores—will soak up water and hold it.

That much is obvious. But there is one mistake people commonly make when thinking about how soils drain, and it is at the root of the oft-repeated but totally false advice to put gravel at the bottom of a container to help it drain. It doesn't, because water does not move well from small pores to large ones.

Water has surface tension. It likes sticking to itself and to objects. Think of a water droplet that hangs onto the faucet after you have turned the water off. It is sitting there, with nothing but one *huge* pore space below it, and yet it doesn't fall. Touch your finger to it, however, and that water will quickly run off the faucet and down your hand. Things with small pores have lots of surface area for water to stick to, so stick to it it does rather than moving off to larger pores below or around it. So water will usually move from materials with large pores—like gravel—into materials with small pores, like clay, not the other way around. This is why we use towels to dry ourselves off rather than marbles, relying on the small pore spaces in the towel to wick the water from the great empty spaces of our skin. So if you put rocks in the bottom of a container, they do not draw water off of the finer textured soil above it. Instead, the water stays in the fine-textured soil, unable to drain away because the pores below it are too large.

So, when constructing a rock garden either mix all soil materials together thoroughly—so water can drain smoothly through pores of all the same size—or use materials with smaller pores (clay, organic matter) on the bottom where they can soak up the excess water from the materials on the top. This, combined with the need to keep the crowns of rock garden plants nice and dry, leads to the recommendation that whatever you make your soil mix out of, you should top it with a nice layer of fine gravel or coarse grit mulch, letting the water drain quickly from the soil surface to the ground below.

Depth of soil matters too. A simple experiment can demonstrate this: Take a regular rectangular kitchen sponge, get it totally saturated with water, then hold it horizontally and let it drip until gravity has pulled out as much water as it can. The remaining water is held in the pores of the sponge and won't drain away. Until, that is, you turn the sponge into a vertical position—suddenly the water will collect in the pores at the bottom of the sponge and more will run out. This applies mostly to rock gardening in containers where depth of soil is limited. Deeper pots will provide better drainage at the soil surface than a shallower pot that holds the same amount of soil. This effect then interacts with another factor—that once water has drained away as much as it can, it then leaves the soil primarily by evaporating from the soil surface, which will happen faster from shallower soils with more area exposed to the air. So deeper containers are usually better and easier to grow rock garden plants in than shallow ones, as they drain moisture away from the soil surface faster, but will then hold deeper water longer where the deep plant roots can reach it.

In an ideal world, you would have your plants sitting on a very dry, well-drained soil surface, but provide them the opportunity to send down roots to moisture below. This imitates the situation where many alpine plants grow, in coarse rocky soil but often with a constant supply of water flowing under them from melting snow and ice higher up the mountain. To some degree nature does this for you, as simple gravity will pull water from the soil surface down deeper, so the soil gets wetter the deeper you go. You can emphasize this effect by using larger particles at the soil surface and smaller ones deeper in the bed. Or even go to the most extreme of this in the technique recommended by rock gardening genius Peter Korn of Sweden, who has built raised beds of sand in a natural bog. The base of the bed is constantly saturated, the top dry, and plants can grow their roots down to find their preferred spot in between. The key to this working is using a material (coarse sand, grit) that is sufficiently coarse so that it won't wick the water up from the bog to the surface via capillary action. Lacking a natural bog, a buried pond liner at the bottom of a bed can create the same effect.

It is usually recommended to mix together a combination of different materials to make rock garden soil. The idea is to combine sand, grit, gravel, and maybe even a little clay or topsoil to provide a mixture of different pore sizes: large pores that ensure good drainage and oxygenation of roots, and small ones to hold a little more water for dry times. A formula I've heard from many excellent rock gardeners is one-third soil, one-third sand, and one-third grit or gravel. This is a good place to start, though the formula doesn't seem to be critical. Many gardeners I know use simply one material—sand or grit mostly—to make beds that grow plants beautifully.

Organic matter is generally not a good thing. Again, if you are a vegetable gardener this may sound strange, because for the rest of the garden, adding organic matter like compost is the magic cure-all for improving soil. But organic matter has lots of tiny pores, holding water like a sponge, and so is particularly unacceptable at the soil surface in the rock garden. Deeper in the bed it is better, but there another factor comes into play: organic matter breaks down. Build a new raised bed with lots of organic matter in the lower layers and over time all that organic matter will finish decomposing, causing the bed to slowly collapse.

SITING: GIVING THE WATER SOMEWHERE TO GO

Whatever the soil mix you use, the best pore size in the world will be useless if there isn't a way for the water to drain out. If you have heavy, soggy soil that tends to flood, digging a hole and filling it with coarse gravel will simply give you a little swimming pool full of coarse gravel. Raised beds, containers, or plantings on slopes are all ways to keep your mass of soil sitting somewhere that allows the excess water to flow away somewhere else. Besides being essential for good drainage, raised beds or other ways of

raising the elevation are important aesthetically for rock gardens. The tiny plants are best appreciated when you don't have to bend down so far to see them, and a lot of flat little plants in a flat little garden can be frankly a bit boring.

ACIDITY AND ALKALINITY

Aside from the physical structure and drainage of the alpine bed, there are chemical considerations, most importantly the pH, a measure of the acidity of the soil. The pH level is measured on a scale ranging from 0 to 14, with 7 being the neutral point (neither acidic nor alkaline), 0 being the most acidic, and 14 being the most alkaline. The pH level in the soil determines a lot about how a soil behaves chemically, most importantly how available certain elements are for plant roots to absorb. In alkaline soils, for example, iron is tightly chemically bound to the soil particles, so plants can't access it, leading to iron deficiencies. In highly acidic soils iron is very available but other elements less so, and aluminum becomes so freely available that it can result in aluminum toxicities. Plants that are native to different soil types have evolved to thrive in those soils, dealing efficiently with shortages of some elements and handling potentially toxic excesses of another. Most plants are fairly adaptable to a reasonable range of different soil pH and the vast majority of plants will grow best in soil that is neutral to slightly acidic, but some species that have adapted to extreme soil pH will demand similar conditions to thrive in the garden.

A raised bed lets excess water drain away.

PLANTS FOR ACID CONDITIONS

alpine snowbells (*Soldanella* species)

bluets (*Houstonia* species)

Chinese gentian (*Gentiana sino-ornata* and related hybrids)

heaths (*Calluna* species)

heathers (*Erica* species)

rhododendrons, dwarf species and cultivars (*Rhododendron*)

PLANTS FOR ALKALINE CONDITIONS

baby's breath (*Gypsophila* species)

blue broom (*Erinacea pungens*)

candytufts (*Iberis* species)

chalk milkwort (*Polygala calcarea*)

saxifrages, silver-leaved species (*Saxifraga*)

woodruffs (*Asperula* species)

In nature, two main factors determine the acidity of a soil. Rainfall is a big one. Water moving through the soil leaches out minerals like calcium and tends to make soil increasingly acidic. So places like rain forests and wetter climates in general tend to have acidic soils. Drier climates don't have the leaching effect of rain so tend to have alkaline soils. The other big factor is the bedrock that is the source of the soil to begin with. I grew up in

Ohio where soils are mostly quite acidic, but there is a little strip of limestone bedrock running through the state producing very alkaline soils. In the United Kingdom, another rainy climate that would generally produce acidic soils, there is also a lot of alkaline bedrock—most famously chalk (which is what makes those cliffs of Dover so white), producing alkaline soils. The preferences of rock garden plants in terms of acidic or alkaline soil are varied. True alpines will be adapted to either alkaline or acidic conditions depending on the chemical composition of the particular mountains they evolved on, while the many excellent rock garden plants that come not from mountaintops but from semi-arid steppe climates around the world will tend to be more alkaline adapted.

In a regular garden you are more or less stuck with the soil that your local bedrock and rainfall patterns have given you, particularly if you have highly alkaline soils. Rock gardens, on the other hand, are endlessly customizable, largely because of their small size. Trying to dig a big enough bed and filling it with peat to keep a large rhododendron happy when you have limestone bedrock is a massive logistical challenge; however, building a small raised bed or filling a container with a soil mix that has just the right acidic soil for a collection of heaths is quite easy. So research the soil preferences of the plants you want to grow, and consider building different beds—some with limestone, some without—to accommodate the full range of plant preferences.

FERTILITY

I've got a confession: I've never fertilized my rock gardens, except occasionally plants growing in containers. Rock garden plants are extremely thrifty and excess fertility can result in loose, unattractive growth. If you have included some topsoil in your mix, it will usually provide plenty of nutrition; most plants will send long roots down through the raised, well-drained portion of your rock garden to the regular soil below to extract additional nutrients. The only situation where you are likely to need to fertilize is for plants in the restricted confines of a container, such as if you are growing in a totally sterile, nutrient-free bed like one made out of pure sand, or if you particularly want to hurry on the growth and expansion of your plants. If you decide to fertilize, whether with an organic or synthetic fertilizer, use it at no more than half the rate recommended on the package. Apply it when plants are coming into active growth, usually the spring or early summer, so they'll be able to use it most effectively.

SOIL IN THE SHADE

One exception to almost everything I've said about soil is the shady rock garden. Purists might say that a shady rock garden is a contradiction in terms. Certainly, since true alpine plants are native above the tree line, none of them are naturally adapted to a woodland garden, but there are many tiny, beautiful woodland treasures from hepaticas to cyclamen to mini hostas that are beautifully displayed and appreciated in a rock garden in the shade. However, where a true alpine will be happiest with rocky mulch that keeps the soil surface dry, most woodland plants grow quite differently, and grow best with the soil covered by a thick layer of slowly decomposing leaf litter. They often have very shallow root systems—to avoid competing with the thick network of tree roots—and frequently form symbiotic relationships with the soil fungi that are abundant in forest soils to supplement their own root systems. Depending on the trees you are planting under, however, thick leaf cover can easily smother tiny plants and kill them, particularly if they pile up directly on the crown of the plant. Collecting and shredding the leaves helps reduce their smothering capabilities, and it is a good idea to push thick leaves away from the crowns of plants.

MATERIALS FOR ROCK GARDEN SOIL

There are many alternatives you can consider in putting together a rock garden soil mix, and many different ones will work very well as long as they meet the basic requirement of good drainage. What you choose to use will depend on many factors. Perhaps most important is to consider a material that is made or mined locally. If you have sand or gravel mines, concrete plants, or other industries using or producing sand or gravel nearby, you should be able to buy the materials you want at much lower costs than if you purchase bagged sand or gravel from a regular retail store. You'll also be much kinder on the environment. A bag of sand or gravel at a chain hardware or building supply store has been shipped from mines to warehouses to more warehouses before winding up on the shelf. Local sourcing will limit the carbon footprint of your materials.

TUFA

Tufa, not to be confused with hypertufa (the concrete-y stuff popular for making faux-stone troughs), is particularly wonderful for rock gardens. The stone is very lightweight and porous and many rock garden plants can grow right out onto the surface of the rock itself, so tufa is a growing medium as well as being beautiful and structural. When happy, some plants will seed directly into the tufa rock, although it is all but impossible to transplant directly onto the rock. Tucking plants into the spaces between two chunks of tufa works well to get plants established, and many gardeners will drill a narrow hole, a couple of centimeters wide, which they can then plant into.

Tufa can be expensive to buy. But if you are lucky enough to live in a region where it occurs naturally, you can often get it for almost nothing, particularly if you know farmers. In northwestern Ohio tufa is common and works its way to the surface of farm fields, so farmers have to haul it out so they can plow—meaning you can often pick up a truckload for a song. The best way to find a source (for this and many other materials for building rock gardens) is to join a local rock gardening society. The experienced rock gardeners will know all the best sources for cheap rock, sand, and gravel; and gardeners are, as a species, generous and happy to share their knowledge with newcomers.

SAND

Sand is very popular for growing rock plants. Championed by Peter Korn, who grows almost exclusively in pure sand, it is a good growing medium and holds water surprisingly well. When I talked to rock gardeners in Denver, Colorado, where rainfall is minimal and regular irrigation is required to garden, they said they had originally shied away from sand as they thought it wouldn't hold enough water for their dry climate, but were proved wrong

Saxifraga 'Peach Melba' growing on a piece of tufa.

when they tried it out. There are several different types of sand, and not all are good for building rock gardens. The best is sharp sand, which is made up of jagged, irregular particles that do not pack as tightly and leave more of that wonderful pore space for roots to grow in. Beach sand, in contrast, has been smoothed by the waves and so tends to pack tightly, making it a poor growing medium. I generally like the coarse sand sold to be added as part of concrete, as it tends to be chunky and irregular with large particles. One

type of sand you might be able to find quite cheaply in cold climates is road salt sand. Contrary to the name, it contains no salt (though double-double check that this is true in your region); rather it is the sand that is applied to roads to prevent cars form slipping on ice when temperatures get too cold for regular road salt to melt the ice. It is inexpensive and really a very nice growing medium.

Gravel with pieces of varying size can be quite attractive.

GRIT

Grit is rock particles of a size in between gravel and sand. The most widely available form of grit, at least in rural areas and increasingly in more urban ones with the current rage for backyard poultry, is chicken grit. Chickens strangely enough need to eat rocks to help them digest their food, and chicken grit contains nicely sized, coarse particles that fit loosely together for lots of pore space. The larger grit sizes make wonderful mulch, especially for the tiniest plants and small container gardens where a regular gravel mulch might be too large. Be aware that crushed oyster shells are sold for feeding to chickens as well, and are great provided you want the alkaline conditions they'll produce.

GRAVEL

Gravel is usually defined as rock chunks bigger than sand but smaller than 2½ inches in diameter, and covers a wide range of different sizes, shapes, colors, and minerals. What you will find for sale will either be pea gravel (with smooth, rounded pieces), or crushed gravel, which is rougher and more jagged in form. After crushing, the gravel is put through a sieve and the large pieces are sold as quarter-ten gravel, and the fines that go through the sieve are called quarter-minus. The main use for gravel in the rock garden is as a surface mulch; there the larger pieces of pea gravel or quarter-ten crushed gravel are generally best and will look the most natural if the color matches that of the rocks you are using in the garden. Gravel by itself doesn't usually hold enough water for most plants, but the finer pieces of quarter-minus gravel can be an excellent addition to heavier soil for drainage, especially in particularly rainy climates. Often nice in that regard though highly variable is road or driveway gravel, very inexpensive gravel that is usually mixed with sand, grit, and even sometimes clay, providing a mixture of pore sizes.

ARTIFICIAL MATERIALS

There are several man-made materials, either special ceramic particles or slate stone heated to the point where it puffs up like popcorn, marketed under names like Permatill and Turface. The results in both cases are individual particles in the grit-to-gravel size range which fit together loosely to form large pores and excellent drainage, but have very small pores within each individual particle that can hold some water. Turface, as the name implies, is used extensively in growing turf for sport fields, and is really excellent stuff. A bit on the pricey side, it grows plants beautifully either on its own or when mixed with other (cheaper) materials. Expanded slate materials are most widely used as media for green roofs, usually mixed with some compost and other soil materials. Like Turface it makes an excellent growing medium for rock plants, with a nearly perfect combination of great drainage and some water retention. If you can find a local company that installs green roofs, you should be able to buy some of their roof soil medium at a very reasonable cost. The Permatill brand of expanded slate is hugely popular and commonly available in the southeastern United States—every gardener I talk to there swears by it—but can be hard to find in other areas.

LEAF MOLD

For true woodland plants, thick leaf loam is their natural and perfect home. Thick leaf litter takes time to develop, and unless you have mature woodland on your property you will probably be starting from scratch in developing a nice woodland soil for your plants. Luckily, in many communities people rake up their leaves in the fall and then put them out to be collected by a municipal trash or composting service, so—especially if you have or can borrow a truck—it is easy to simply drive around and collect up as many leaves as you want. When I lived in a rural area where people dealt with the

Heat-expanded slate is the basis of these berms at the J C Raulston Arboretum in North Carolina, providing the sharp drainage to keep agaves and other dry-loving plants happy in a rainy climate.

leaves on their own properties, I would simply drive to nearby neighborhoods in the fall and grab as many bags as I wanted. People certainly gave me odd looks, but I've never had anyone complain about me taking what they think of as trash. Unless the leaves are very small and fine-textured, shredding them before applying them to the garden is the best way to avoid smothering small, choice plants and to jump-start the decomposition process. If you have a choice of leaves, choose oak. Oak leaves are *very* slow to decompose, and so form a wonderful almost peat-like layer of organic matter as they slowly, slowly break down, producing a perfect home for many of the pickiest woodlanders.

PEAT

For a standard rock garden peat is generally not a great idea, as it holds too much moisture. But for a shady rock garden it is very helpful—acidifying soil and mimicking many of the attributes of the bottom layer of decomposing leaves that woodland plants are adapted to. However, peat has become environmentally controversial in recent years. Peat takes centuries to develop so it is a finite, essentially nonrenewable resource. In northern Europe that resource has been heavily exploited for a long time, for fuel and even building material as well as for horticultural uses. In North America, however, the massive peat bogs of Canada have been barely touched, and the peat harvesting companies there have an excellent history of replanting and restoring bogs after harvesting. The biggest environmental concern for peat and peat replacements like coconut fiber is honestly the fossil fuels used to ship the materials to your garden. So if you live in the North, relatively close to where peat is harvested, it is probably a more environmentally sound choice than coconut fiber. Though of course nothing is going to beat homemade leaf mold in terms of a small carbon footprint.

Choosing a soil mix for a rock garden can be overwhelming, as there are many different materials to choose from, but the good news is that long list of options really indicates that you have a lot of leeway in choosing materials for your rock garden. Every rock gardener I've talked to does something a little different, and they all have excellent results. Start with something you can easily get locally, make sure it drains well, and don't worry about it too much.

Containers

Rock garden and alpine plants are particularly well suited to growing in containers. The small plant size allows you to grow a diversity of plants even in a small container and many rock garden plants are quite drought tolerant, always a plus in containers which can dry out so quickly. Additionally, the smallest and most exquisite plants can get lost in the larger garden, so a container is a perfect way to elevate them closer to eye level while framing and highlighting their particular beauty. Containers also have a practical aspect, as they can be moved around. So if, for example, lewisias rot out in your summer rains, you can move the container they are growing in under the eave of the house during their post-flowering resting period to keep them dry and happy. Containers are also of course perfect for the gardener without a garden, squeezing plants onto an apartment balcony or rooftop. The fad in container planting in recent years has been toward lush, mixed containers with a few large, full annuals in the so-called thriller, filler, spiller formula. This gives you maybe three or four different species in a container. They're beautiful but honestly getting a bit boring. A small alpine container or trough can easily pack in twice that many species with a wide range of forms, seasonal color, and winter interest: a whole landscape in a pot.

TYPES OF CONTAINERS

Rock gardeners usually use the word *trough* to describe their container plantings. The original troughs were carved from stone and used to hold water for farm animals. These large, heavy, beautiful containers were co-opted for growing alpines and their form and aesthetic have dominated container rock gardening ever since, but troughs are by no means the only way you can grow rock garden plants in a container. Any container that can hold soil and has holes for water to drain out the bottom can be used.

Hypertufa

Real stone troughs are hard to come by, very expensive, heavy, and difficult to move. They are also incredibly beautiful. If you can find—and afford—stone troughs, by all means use them in your garden. Far more common are hypertufa "stone" troughs. Hypertufa is a man-made stone-like substance that takes its name from natural tufa, a lightweight, porous limestone rock. Hypertufa is similarly lightweight and porous and can be very attractive, particularly once it has aged in the garden and acquired a patina of moss or lichen.

Hypertufa is a variant of concrete. Both are made out of Portland cement, a rather magical powder that when mixed with water, solidifies and hardens. To make concrete, the cement is mixed with sand and gravel, which makes it heavy, very strong, and used for nearly everything in modern construction from sidewalks to foundations to bridges. To make hypertufa, you use the same Portland cement, but instead of sand and

Although real stone troughs are undeniably handsome, they're both scarce and expensive.

gravel you add peat and perlite, which results in a much lighter-weight, somewhat porous finished product. Perhaps most importantly, the peat and perlite change the overall appearance of the hypertufa so it looks more like stone and less like concrete. You can really add many different things to the mix: shredded paper (to make papercrete), additional peat, or vermiculite in place of perlite. Different materials will change the aesthetic

HOW TO MAKE A HYPERTUFA CONTAINER

Though easy and rewarding, making hypertufa is messy. The finished product will cure the best in a cool, shaded spot, so choose your workspace accordingly. Be sure to wear thick gloves and a mask to protect yourself from the caustic, irritating cement.

MATERIALS

1 part Portland cement (not premixed concrete)

1 part peat, composted bark, or other fibrous organic matter

1 part perlite or vermiculite

1 cup concrete reinforcing fibers per 5 gallons total mix

INSTRUCTIONS

1 In a large plastic tub or wheelbarrow, mix all ingredients together. Slowly add water while stirring until the mix is about the consistency of cottage cheese. If you take a fistful and squeeze, it should hold together in a ball. If more than a few drops of water ooze out when you squeeze, it is too wet.

2 Once your mix is made, form it into a container. You can smear it over a mound of sand or a container covered with plastic; pack it between two different-sized cardboard boxes; or build a custom mold out of sheets of Styrofoam. Be creative. Just be sure to poke drainage holes in the bottom.

3 Once the container has been formed, cover it loosely with plastic and let cure.

4 After about 36 hours, your container should be partially set and can be removed, carefully, from the mold. At this stage the hypertufa hasn't reached full hardness, and you can, if you wish, texture the sides with a wire brush or chisel. Rewrap your container in plastic, and let it sit for another 3 weeks to finish curing and reach maximal strength.

5 Finally, you need to leach any lingering lime from your trough to avoid creating an extremely alkaline soil when you plant it up. Do this by letting it sit out in the rain for several months or by hosing the container down twice a day for a week.

For most gardeners, hypertufa troughs are an affordable, attractive, and easy-to-make alternative to stone.

and characteristics of the final product. The standard formula will produce attractive and functional hypertufa, but if you get into making these containers it is well worth playing around with different materials and ratios to see what you get and what appeals to you the most. The look can be further customized by adding cement dyes to the mix, embedding distinctive stones or other materials, and aging them in a cool, moist spot to encourage the growth of mosses and lichens.

Hypertufa and the various hypertufa variants are not as strong as regular concrete; their porous nature allows water to get in, which can then freeze in the winter causing it to crack, so it is a good idea to add something to the mix to make it stronger. The two standard options are fiberglass fibers, which you simply add to the mix, and embedding wire into the form—chicken wire works nicely and is easy to shape. Both work well and a combination will be the absolute strongest, though that will only be required if you are making a very large container with very thin walls.

left › This wire basket makes an elegant, up-cycled container for a saxifrage.

right › You can get creative even with ordinary flowerpots.

Found and up-cycled containers

As I said, almost anything can be used to make a container. I once planted up the drawers of a filing cabinet, which I rather enjoyed but was not to the taste of many garden visitors. Obviously the biggest consideration here will be your personal taste. The more whimsical your gardening style, the more likely you are to get into planting up unexpected finds from thrift stores; with careful looking and a design eye, you can find seriously beautiful containers in very unexpected places. There are a couple of practical concerns to keep in mind when using nontraditional containers. First, of course, is drainage. If there aren't holes, you are going to have to drill some. The second matter is simply the size of the container. Too small or too shallow, and it will not be able to hold much soil mass—making it very prone to drying out. In general, these less-than-ideal containers will work best with plants like cacti, sempervivums, and other succulents that can handle a limited root run and the occasional water shortage.

In addition to growing sempervivums beautifully, old shoes used as containers are useful for annoying uptight gardeners who don't like having fun with their container choices.

left › *Tetraneuris* growing in a natural stone crack at Denver Botanic Gardens.

above › **Double bloodroot** (*Sanguinaria canadensis* f. *multiplex* 'Plena') blooming in what amounts to a container between rocks.

Natural (or nearly natural) rock crevices

Sometimes natural rock will form a little container than can hold some soil, which can be quite lovely. These work best if the stone is something porous like natural tufa, which will allow water to drain out of the cavity of the rock. If not, you'll need to drill a drainage hole unless the depression is very shallow so the quantity of water held isn't so great that it won't be able to evaporate away quite quickly. If you nearly have a shape that will hold some soil, you can augment the natural form of the stone either by carving out a bigger opening or building up walls. A little clay can be shaped to form a small wall to hold some soil, and can then be disguised by pressing moss onto the surface or planting something spreading to cover it; on larger stones, you can use cement or mortar to attach smaller stones to build a space that will hold soil.

Flat surfaces

One of the most unusual sorts of containers is not a container at all. Soil can be mounded directly on top of a flat rock, a tabletop, a patio, or almost anything else. The final result can be incredibly striking. You'd think all the soil would wash away with the first rain or watering, but when the arrangement is put together the right way, this problem is pretty easy to avoid. The first key is to use a soil mix that holds together—standard peat-based potting medium does this very well, and adding some garden soil will also help. Using these heavier, water-holding soils will limit the number of true alpines you can grow, but the effect is dramatic enough to be worth it. The other key is to plant the edges thickly with something that will root in and hold the soil in place, come rain or garden hose. Sempervivums, the groundcover veronicas, phloxes, small sedums, and creeping mint (*Mentha requienii*, formerly *Valantia muralis*) work particularly well, though really anything that will grow and fill in fairly quickly will work. Water carefully and protect from torrential rains until the edges get thoroughly rooted in, and then you are good to go.

Small containers and plunge beds

Small containers are well suited for displaying rock garden plants and are required if you are going to be taking specimens to a show. Growing a plant

Take inspiration from the world of bonsai, and explore using flat surfaces to grow alpines.

Primula marginata blooming happily in a pot in a plunge bed at the Royal Botanic Garden Edinburgh.

singly in a pot allows you to customize conditions to grow an absolutely perfect specimen of that particular species or variety, and makes it very easy to move them to display in full flower in a special spot in the garden or house. Small containers, however, have practical difficulties. They dry out, over-heat, and freeze quickly and easily, lacking the mass to insulate them from sudden changes. The classic solution to this problem is a plunge bed. Essentially this is a large sandbox, either on the ground or built up on a bench in an alpine house or greenhouse, and you plunge the pots into the sand so it comes up to the top of the container. Kept moist, the sand prevents rapid drying and insulates the pot from sudden temperature changes. In addition to being perfect for growing plants for show, plunge beds are absolutely invaluable as holding spaces for plants you recently bought or propagated but haven't had time to plant in the garden. I think most of us have had the experience of coming home from the nursery with a tray full of goodies, only to kill the choicest of them by not getting them planted in time. Shove your new plants into the plunge bed, and they'll hold beautifully until you are ready to get them in ground.

PRACTICAL ASPECTS OF ROCK GARDENING IN A CONTAINER

Lovely as containers are, gardening in them can require a little more care than growing in the open garden, and there are some practical matters you need to take into account.

Soil

Soil for containers is a little different from soil in the main rock garden. Many true alpine plants have deep root systems, allowing them to grow down through the very well-drained soil of your main bed and into the wetter layers below. The limited size of a container makes that impossible, so you are going to be better off using a more moisture-retentive soil mix. The general principles outlined in the soil section still apply, but I'd generally recommend adjusting your mixtures for containers to hold a little more water. For example, if you use a mix of sand and grit in the main garden, consider just using sand in your containers, or even adding some organic matter like a standard peat potting mix. Just as for in-ground plantings, be sure to top off your container mixture with a layer of gravel to keep the crowns of plants dry.

Fertilization

Again rock garden plants in general grow and look better in lean, low-fertility conditions, and excessive fertilization can lead to loose, unattractive growth. While roots of plants in the open rock garden can reach down to extract nutrients from deep in the soil, containerized plants are stuck with limited root systems and will do better with a little supplemental fertilizer now and then. Whether you choose an organic or synthetic fertilizer is up to you, but whatever you use, apply it at a reduced rate—perhaps half of what the fertilizer's label recommends—and then keep an eye on how the plants respond. If your tight buns start growing too lush and loose, cut back the fertilizer next time around.

Overwintering

In cold climates winter is the most difficult time to handle containers, and the smaller the container the more of a problem it is. The issue here is how exposed the roots of the plants are to sudden changes of temperature. The mass of soil that makes up the ground or a large bed has a lot of thermal mass, meaning that it warms and cools slowly. While air temperatures can swing rapidly, the soil—even if only an inch or two down—slowly cools in the fall and then slowly warms in the spring, insulating plant roots from sudden changes and the harshest temperatures. A small container, however, doesn't have the mass to provide that insulation, so roots in it will face much more extreme conditions.

One solution is to use extremely winter-hardy plants. As a rule of thumb, plants that are hardy to one or two USDA hardiness zones colder than where you garden can hack a winter in an exposed container. The other option is to move the container somewhere to give it more protection. You can mass containers against the north wall of the house, packing them in with something like fallen leaves to add extra insulation. These conditions overwinter plants nicely, but also make ideal nesting grounds for mice and other rodents. So if you have a problem with them in your garden or have containers of tasty bulbs, you should cover the containers with hardware cloth to keep the nibblers out. An unheated or minimally heated garage or shed is a perfect place to overwinter containers. Ideally, the temperature should stay right around freezing, cold enough to keep the plants dormant so they don't need light, but warm enough so they won't suffer any winter damage. Other options, if you have them, are cold frames or a cool greenhouse. What you don't want to do is bring them inside to a sunny windowsill. Indoors it will be warm enough for the plants to break dormancy and start trying to grow, but there isn't nearly enough light coming in even the sunniest window on a short winter day to keep the plants happy.

But what about huge containers you can't easily move to a sheltered spot? Well, the good thing is that the bigger the container, the more soil mass, and the less of a problem winter is. As a sheer practical matter, if a container is too big for me to move easily, I deem it big enough to come through the winter fine and that seems to work out well. Don't put plants that are borderline hardy in a container you won't be protecting over the winter, but if the container is quite large, you don't need to be concerned.

One last consideration is the container itself. Many ceramic pots will crack if left out through the freezes and thaws of winter, so move them into

right › **Tiny** *Erodium chamaedryoides* **'Charm' is perfectly adapted to life in a container.**

far right ›
So-called Long Tom pots are taller and narrower than standard pots, which make them ideal for alpines that form a carrot-like taproot, like auriculas.

a situation like an unheated garage. If you are planning to leave a container outdoors for the winter, ask before you purchase if it will be able to survive those conditions.

Plant choices for containers

Containers, especially very small containers, generally provide harsher conditions than the regular garden. Soil dries out faster, root run is limited, and soil temperatures fluctuate more rapidly and reach greater extremes of heat and cold. So usually it is a good idea to stick with the tougher, more reliable plants for your containers, and keep the real drama queens in the ground. The exception is if you are using the container to significantly modify the climate for that particular plant, like planting in a refrigerated container or moving a plant under a sheltering eave to keep off excess rain. Most rock garden plants, however, adapt very well to life in containers.

Aesthetically, another range of consideration comes into play. Containers are small, so small plants work best in them. Rapidly spreading plants can quickly become a problem in a small container. The reality is that even the most miniature of plants will tend to outgrow a small container after a number of years. Even tiny plants keep growing and developing, getting bigger year after year as shrubs grow, bulbs divide, and perennials add more eyes. For that reason, I think container plantings really are best treated as fairly short-term. Plan on ripping them apart and redoing them every few years. For instance, consider using smaller containers as little nurseries to grow-on new plants for a few years until they're big enough to move out into a larger container or the regular garden. I particularly love using dwarf conifers this way. The only way I can afford dwarf conifers is buying them as tiny little rooted cuttings or new grafts, and putting something that small in the garden seems like a waste. But tucked into a container they look perfect. Then once they've grown on for a few years and are starting to get too big for the container, they're ready for the main garden. Similarly, one or two bulbs of a rare species of narcissus can be highlighted in a container until they have multiplied enough to be ready to make a small drift in the garden. Containers are also perfect for impulse purchases—those beautiful plants that I bought because I couldn't live without them but that I don't really know where to place in the garden or maybe even how well they will grow for me. A container makes a nice temporary home while I get everything figured out.

ROCKS IN CONTAINERS

As in the main garden, stones are far from required in a container but they are beautiful and help provide lots of interest. The small size of containers and their more ephemeral nature make them a perfect space to experiment with unusual rocks, such as colorful and unusual minerals. Doing a whole rock garden with pink rock or blue-veined stones feels to me like it would be a bit much, but limited down to the size of a container I think the brighter

colors and more eye-catching stones work better and are easier to design around. Besides, of course, being dramatically easier on the pocketbook. But you by no means need to invest in expensive stones to make a beautiful container. A couple of years ago I attended a North American Rock Garden Society winter study weekend where the speaker gave a demonstration on planting troughs, and for rocks he merely walked outside and grabbed some stones from the edge of the parking lot. Combined with plants, they looked spectacular. You can even add flat rocks and create a mini crevice garden.

Containers aren't difficult to plant, and they're a great place to experiment. It is easy to rip apart a container that you don't like, so they're a perfect place to try your most out-there ideas and give them a trial run before setting them loose on the whole garden. Add in the wide range of interesting and off-the-beaten-path things you can grow plants in, and your containers can be some of the most exciting and interesting parts of your garden.

Climate

Researching this book I've been traveling
all over to visit great gardens and gardeners,
which has been tons of fun. So many of the
people I've talked to are terrific gardeners
who I really respect, and who I'd *really* like
to have think well of me. With embarrassing
frequency, however, I visit a garden in an
unfamiliar climate and start losing my
composure over some plant. I ask what it is,
say I've never seen anything so marvelous,
how beautiful, I wonder if I can grow it,
can I please, please, please beg a cutting or
some seeds? My hosts invariably are polite,
telling me the name and cheerfully offering
me cuttings or even digging up a chunk. I'm
glowing with pleasure at my rare, new prize,

Plants from regions that experience intense sunlight, like *Acantholimon echinus,* grow tighter and produce more flowers when you can provide similar conditions.

only then to drive around town and realize—the plant is everywhere. It is, in short, the commonest, most unexciting plant in the area. And my hosts, instead of being impressed with my plant knowledge, are thinking, "He doesn't know this?" This sort of display of regional plant ignorance is a constant danger to the traveling gardener and is a great illustration of the enormous role climate plays in gardening. A tough, easy, reliable mainstay in one climate can be an exquisite, difficult rarity in another, and vice versa.

Understanding your local climate and how the plants respond to it is key to success in any sort of gardening. Plants that are naturally adapted to thrive in the conditions of your garden will be easy to grow, requiring little fuss or special care and rewarding you with big payoffs in healthy growth, abundant flowers, and beautiful forms. As much fun in a very different way is growing plants that *aren't* naturally adapted to your climate. There is a real pleasure in finding just the right microclimate or making just the right adjustment to your conditions to allow something you never thought you could grow to thrive in your garden. As a rock gardener, you will have ample opportunity to grow both sorts of plants. The sheer diversity of plants that

For northern gardeners, considering the impact of cold winters dominates planting choices.

can be grown in a rock garden means that wherever you garden, you'll be able to find lots of plants that thrive easily. At the same time, the small size of rock garden plants makes it very possible to find and construct special spots and conditions to grow a whole range of plants that normally would be impossible.

TAKING THE COLD: WINTER HARDINESS

You can always identify gardeners like myself who live in a chilly, northern climate, because the first question we ask about an interesting new plant is always, "Is it hardy?" Winter cold is a major determining factor in how well plants can grow, and one gardeners focus on a lot, perhaps because the results of not surviving winter cold are so dramatic. Other climatic mismatches tend to cause a plant to slowly decline or fail to thrive. Death by cold is unambiguous. Spring comes, the snow melts, and bam, no more plant. Luckily for cold-climate rock gardeners, most classic rock garden plants hail from the icy tops of mountains and are extremely tolerant of cold temperatures. But winter hardiness is a complex matter, and a plant that can take your temperatures might not survive your winter for other reasons, because winter hardiness—or the lack thereof—is the result of multiple factors interacting.

Temperature

The major factor in determining winter hardiness is, of course, temperature. That is the idea behind the zone maps produced by the United States Department of Agriculture, which divide the country into numbered zones based on the average winter low temperatures over the last 30 years. I live in USDA zone 5b, meaning my winters average a low between -10°F and -15°F. The most powerful tool you have to raise your winter temperatures is usually your house. Houses, especially old, poorly insulated ones, leak warmth out into the ground around them, so plants right against the side of the house will be protected from the most extreme cold. Aspect has a big effect as well, but a complex one. Southern exposures will get the most sun and warmth during the day, but that can be a mixed blessing, as that added warmth vanishes quickly once the sun goes down and temperatures really

This lovely little greenhouse in Quebec, Canada, is practical and beautiful.

start dropping. That extra heat can fool plants into waiting too long to go into dormancy or breaking into growth too early in the spring.

The other way to modify the temperature your plants are experiencing is to build some kind of protection over them. The most elaborate of these is a heated greenhouse, which gives you the ultimate (if quite expensive) control over winter temperatures. Simpler, less pricey solutions like cold frames or other unheated coverings can have a big impact as well, particularly in protecting plants from short, extreme cold snaps.

Finally, you can move your plants, something that is easy to do with small rock garden plants, especially those growing in a container like a trough. Slide that container into an unheated garage or other sheltered-but-cool place, and you can easily grow plants better adapted to much warmer climates.

Spring volatility

Plants, even the most winter-hardy ones, are not prepared to withstand cold temperatures all the time. During the summer when they are in active growth, almost all plants would be killed or at least seriously damaged by even a light freeze. As winter comes on, signals like temperature and shortening days tell plants to start shutting down growth, produce antifreeze compounds, shed delicate leaves, go dormant, and start building up to their maximal cold tolerance. In spring, that process goes in reverse as they come out of dormancy and start growing again. In the climates where they evolved, plants have the timing for these processes down pat, building up to full dormancy before the first cold snap and waiting to start growth in the spring until risk of freezes is past.

However, when a plant is growing somewhere with more volatile weather, or in a year with a freak late freeze, growth can start too early and the new fragile leaves or flower buds not adapted to cold can get frozen back. Luckily, most plants for the rock garden are very tolerant of unexpected spring weather. Steppe lands and mountaintops where most rock garden plants originate tend to have quite volatile weather, so plants there are prepared for sudden temperature swings and deal with late spring freezes quite well. Plants from areas with more stable spring temperatures handle late freezes much more poorly.

There are two main ways to avoid damage from late spring freezes. First, site plants in the coldest spot in your garden—the north side of the house or north side of a slope, the spot where the snow and frost linger the longest—if they tend to come into growth too early and get frosted back. That cool microclimate will keep them dormant longer in the spring, delaying growth until the risk of late frosts has passed. The other way is to keep an eye on the weather reports and be prepared to rush out with a bed sheet to cover the plants if a late frost is predicted. This is easiest to do if you grow all the plants that will need protection together, so you can simply throw the cover over one bed and be done rather than having to go through the whole garden to track down the vulnerable plants.

Pleione orchids are not quite hardy outside for John Grimshaw in North Yorkshire, United Kingdom, but he grows them easily by moving the containers to a cool spot indoors for the winter.

Winter and spring wet

Drainage can be nearly as important a factor for winter hardiness as temperature, particularly for rock garden plants that generally hail from steep, rocky soils where excess water drains away quickly. Where I garden in Michigan, spring is *wet*. The snow melts, saturating the soil, and we tend to get plenty of rain, again keeping soil saturated. On top of that, our spring is usually cool and cloudy, so water is slow to evaporate. This makes a particularly lethal combination with winter damage because an odd stem or leaf killed by winter cold provides a perfect point of entry for pathogens that thrive in the cool, wet conditions.

These effects cause huge differences in winter hardiness. At the nursery where I worked in Michigan, we joked about "Denver hardy" plants. I'm good friends with the brilliant plantsmen at Denver Botanic Gardens in Colorado, Panayoti Kelaidis and Mike Kintgen, and they frequently share plants with us here in Michigan. Our average winter low temperatures are the same; however, here in Michigan we get an average of 31 inches of rain a year. In Denver that number is 17 inches. The difference that change in rainfall makes in hardiness is huge, most dramatically with dryland plants and succulents like agaves, yuccas, delospermas, and cacti, but also with all sorts of other plants you might not expect. Despite similar winter temperatures, that difference in moisture makes a huge difference in hardiness.

If you live in a rainy climate, the best thing you can do for winter hardiness in your rock garden is to make sure the soil you use has perfect drainage so all that extra water is carried quickly away. If you are hard-core, you can also build temporary roofs over your plants, preferably with something transparent like polycarbonate, which will let light through. This works, but it is also kind of ugly, which sort of defeats the purpose of a garden in my mind. A more complex and more attractive version of this is an alpine house—I've got more information on that later in this chapter in the moisture section. My personal favorite way is to grow in containers, which can be moved under the eaves of a house or into an unheated shed or garage in the winter to keep excess water off.

> Containers give you the option of growing plants that might not be hardy when planted in the ground in your climate.

Snow cover

Snow is a wonderful insulator; plants nestled under a thick blanket of snow are extremely well protected from the coldest temperatures of winter. Gardeners in cold climates with regular, reliable snow cover are able to grow a whole range of plants that won't survive similar temperatures without the added insulation of snow. Snow is a particularly important factor in the rock garden because small plants can be completely covered, giving them solid insulation that taller trees and shrubs can't benefit from.

If you have regular snow cover, rejoice. If not, a good alternative is to cover beds with a loose layer of cut branches from conifers like pines or spruces. They provide insulation but are loose and open enough that they don't smother the plants or cause them to rot out. Wait, however, until winter has really set in, the ground has frozen, and plants are totally dormant so they won't need light to photosynthesize and keep growing. Obviously this is only possible if you have access to a good supply of evergreen branches to cut. If you celebrate Christmas (or have friends or neighbors who do), Christmas trees are a great source of branches to use in the garden. Another great, less traditional but very effective and reusable option is floating row covers sold for vegetable growers. These thin fabric sheets provide a layer of insulation but are light enough to not smother plants. Whatever covering you use, putting all your most tender plants together in one or two specific beds will make covering them much easier and will require much less material than if you have them scattered all over the garden.

HEAT

Summer heat is a big factor in growing many true alpine plants. Mountaintops are not exactly warm places generally. More importantly, thin air at high altitudes doesn't hold heat, which means that even if temperatures get high during the day, they cool off again dramatically at night. For all plants, high night temperatures are far more damaging than high daytime temps. During the day, plants are making food with their leaves. During the night, with the sun gone they can't photosynthesize, so they have to burn some of that food to keep their biological processes going. Higher temperatures for plants means higher rates of metabolism, so warm nights can cause plants to starve to death.

Excess summer heat is one of the hardest factors to change in a garden. In general, you will be best off understanding and accepting the reality of the summer climate you've been dealt. Northern exposures and shady spots will be cooler in the summer, but alpine plants generally want sun. Water provides evaporative cooling fairly effectively in low-humidity climates, but low humidity usually means cool nights anyway, and misting to cool plants in a hot-humid climate is a recipe for rot.

There are two fairly extreme measures you can take to grow plants that demand cooler temperatures than your climate can provide. One is using straight up air conditioning to cool off a greenhouse or alpine house. The critical thing here is to keep the night temperature cool, so you can save some money by turning the air conditioner off during the day, but it is still a very expensive and not environmentally sensitive way to grow unusual plants. A more labor-intensive but long term much more sustainable and less energy-intensive solution is to go below ground. At depth, soil maintains a steady temperature of about 50°F. The traditional way to make use of this is to create a pit house, a greenhouse sunk below ground. Or, in another way to think of it, a hole in the ground with a greenhouse roof over it. They're not realistic for the vast majority of gardeners, but if you are feeling exceptionally ambitious, they do really work.

MOISTURE

Rainfall determines *so* much of how and what plants will grow in a region. I've always lived and gardened in relatively wet climates, and traveling to significantly drier ones is eye opening. Having plenty of natural moisture is wonderful because you don't have to irrigate regularly, making gardening less labor intensive and more sustainable. But from the point of view of "customizing" your climate, less rainfall gives you more options. It is quite straightforward to add water to a garden, provided you can afford the water bills. It is much more difficult to remove it. Providing superb drainage to let excess water drain away is the first step. Beyond drainage, the only real option for limiting natural rainfall is to do something to keep the rain off. Alpine houses are structures that do essentially that. In its simplest form, an alpine house is an unheated greenhouse with a transparent roof that keeps rain off but lets light in. In warm summer climates, the critical aspect is to ensure that an alpine house does not overheat. Building it as a roof with no walls is an easy way to ensure perfect ventilation and keeps the house from overheating in the summer. If the walls are easy to remove and put back on, the alpine house can double as a greenhouse in the winter.

If you have a dry climate and want to turn it wet, irrigation is obviously the standard answer, though an ecologically fraught one at times. The

climates where gardeners are most inclined to water are, almost by definition, the ones where natural supplies of water are limited and irrigation is of questionable environmental sustainability. Gardening with limited water supplies is a major concern in the American West, and rock gardens are extremely well suited to dryland gardening. True alpines frequently want regular water, but many marvelous plants from steppe and dryland regions of the world work beautifully in a rock garden. The small size of rock gardens also makes them perfect for conserving water. Pack all of your favorite, water-loving alpines into one bed and even if you have to irrigate it regularly, the small size means you'll be able to limit the total amount of water you use.

Short of irrigating, there are other ways to make sure plants get more water. Light shade reduces water needs dramatically, and of course low areas—whether natural or built by you—will collect and hold water longer than positions on the tops or sides of hills. Rubber pond liner is another simple and easy way to make a wetter area in the garden. Most gardeners are familiar with using pond liners to build bogs by filling the liner with soil, but you can create whole gradients of moisture levels by building the soil up higher over the liner so it isn't totally saturated like a bog, but plant roots can still reach down to access a constant supply of water. Whether you rely on natural rainfall or irrigate, these pockets will hold moisture so it can't drain away, keeping water-loving plants happy.

It is important when irrigating to remember that tap water is not the same as rainwater. Rainwater contains minimal amounts of dissolved minerals and is slightly acidic. Tap water varies wildly depending on the source, but it almost always has quite a bit of dissolved minerals and is somewhat alkaline. If you are going to be irrigating regularly, it is important to get your water tested so you know what effect it is going to have on your soil. If you are trying to maintain an acidic bed for plants that demand it and your water is very alkaline, the best option is to save rainwater or use distilled water to avoid raising the soil pH. If you do have to water an acidic bed with alkaline water in a pinch, it won't be the end of the world, especially if you are able to flush away the alkalinity with more pure or acidic water in the future. For example, I water my acidic bogs during dry spells in the summer with my rather alkaline well water, confident that the massive excesses of precipitation in fall through spring will leach away any bad effects.

HUMIDITY

One of the strangest things to me about gardens in dry climates is just how *frequently* they have to be watered. In my garden in Michigan, a good rainfall once every week or two in the summer is plenty to keep plants perfectly happy. But in a dry, dry climate like Colorado, gardeners have to apply much more water, irrigating multiple times per week because it evaporates into the dry air so quickly. So humidity matters. And unfortunately, it is a part of your climate you pretty much just have to accept as-is. You can fairly easily raise humidity (or lower it, with an air conditioner or dehumidifier) in enclosed spaces like a greenhouse, but in the open garden you are largely stuck with what you've got. Shade, windbreaks, and packing plants

Two alpine houses at the Royal Botanic Garden Edinburgh, a very modern one in the front and a more traditional style in the back. Both do the job, but which one is more visually pleasing is a matter of debate.

close together will raise humidity, while ensuring good air movement and keeping plants spaced apart will reduce it, but you can only do so much. Rock garden plants, as a rule, come from areas of low humidity and thin air and generally take dry air with ease, but they will be much more prone to various fungal pathogens like mildews and rusts in humid conditions, so ensuring a free flow of air through the rock garden will help keep them as healthy as possible.

LIGHT

As gardeners, we're used to thinking about sun versus shade. Too much sun is quickly lethal to plants adapted to shade, burning leaves and drying plants up. Too little sun tends to cause less dramatic effects—plants grow looser and taller, flower less, and tend to slowly decline. For rock gardens, you need to remember that full sun in one place is not the same as full sun in another. The thin air at high altitudes filters out less of the intensity of the sun, meaning a sunny day on a mountaintop packs quite a bit more of a punch than that at lower altitudes. Similarly, the many great rock garden plants from dry climates live with lots of bright, sunny, cloudless days. This is very different from the conditions in, for example, my garden in Michigan where we average only 71 days of sunny, cloudless weather a year. Even without any shade, my garden simply gets less solar radiation than a garden in a sunnier climate like say, Medford, Oregon, which boasts around 200 sunny days a year.

Theoretically, you could improve light intensity with mirrors or a bright-white painted wall to the south of a bed, but practically speaking there is little you can do to alter the light conditions in your garden other than understanding and accepting it. In Colorado, acantholimons form beautiful, tight mounds and are absolutely loaded with flowers. Even in full sun in Michigan, the exact same plants are looser and less attractive, and flowering is usually sparse. If you don't know anything about a plant, you can get some clues about how much sun it wants from how it looks. In general, plants with very blue, glaucous leaves, or silver, hairy leaves, have those leaf colors as adaptations to reflect excess light to prevent leaves from burning and drying out and will, as a rule, do best in a climate with very intense sun. However, exceptions to that rule abound, so don't write off a beautiful blue or silver leaf without trying it.

Understanding your local climate and knowing when to modify it and when to just embrace it is key to successful gardening. Learning from other gardeners in your region will give you a great basis of knowledge to work with; when you read about or visit gardens in different climates, understanding precisely how their conditions differ from yours will help you figure out how to adapt their plants and practices to the realities of your home garden. And always remember, the rock garden is the perfect place to practice your most extreme climate modifications—the small scale makes it so much more practical than when gardening with larger plants.

I can't leave the topic of climate without giving two pieces of advice.

First, if you really want to grow something, try it. Many times. Even if all the references say it won't thrive where you live. There are many plants that are listed as tender in reference works simply because no one has tried them in a colder place, and many more that will thrive for you even though they haven't done well in gardens that seem similar. When experimenting with new plants, if possible try them in different locations. Sometimes a plant that rots out when grown on the level will thrive when high and dry on the top of a crevice garden, or something that baked in your hot summer will grow happily on the cool, north side of a big stone. So buy, or propagate, a few plants at a time and scatter them around so you can see where they really want to grow.

Second, don't forget to stop and notice the times when the grass is greener on *your* side of the fence. When traveling or seeing pictures of other gardens, it is easy to see all the plants that look so much better than they do in your home garden—or the lovely things that you can't grow at all—while failing to notice the plants that look great in your garden and are missing entirely in another region. The Internet is a great place to get some perspective. When something is looking particularly stunning in your garden, post a picture to a Facebook gardening group or an online horticulture forum, particularly ones with international membership, and watch people around the world drool over plants to which you don't give a second thought. Embrace those plants, embrace your climate, and you'll have a lovely garden and more fun in it.

Getting (and Making) More Plants

163

Nursery beds at Broadleigh Gardens in Somerset, England.

Unless you are very lucky indeed, the selection of rock garden plants at your local garden center is likely to be slim to none. The business of horticulture has gotten bigger, more automated, and more intensive in recent years; and the result is that plants that don't make good cogs in the gears of the horticultural-industrial complex are less and less available. The standard model today is for wholesale growers to produce plants on a huge scale with massive amounts of fertilizer and water to get them to rapidly bulk up to a nice full pot of flowers that will look pretty sitting on a garden center bench. Many if not most of the best alpines and other rock garden plants don't fit that model

because they respond to rich growing conditions by getting loose, leggy, and ugly, and possibly by rotting. And many of the best species simply don't tend to look very good growing in a little nursery pot—they want to stretch out deep roots in the open garden. Others, like daphnes, can grow and bloom beautifully in a large pot at a nursery but resent transplanting once they get big—they really need to be sold as little rooted cuttings that don't look pretty but will thrive in the ground. Because of these limitations, you'll need to look elsewhere for the bulk of the really great plants for a rock garden.

SPECIALTY NURSERIES AND MAIL ORDER

Nurseries focusing on rare and unusual plants have had a pretty rough go of it in the United States in recent years, with many of the best of them going belly-up. But there are still many excellent ones that will be able to provide you with a wide range of exquisite plants. If you are fortunate to have one near you, visiting and shopping in person is always the best, but if not, mail order is an excellent plan B. Shipping plants through the mail is always a bit expensive and hard on the plants, but the small size and compact habit of most plants for the rock garden means that they do tend to travel in a box fairly well and with minimal damage.

When visiting a specialty nursery, or ordering from one, you have to reset your mind a little. Running a specialty nursery is a thankless job. Profits are minimal, hours are long, and consequently, the people foolish enough to start one tend to be a bit, well, odd. In a good way, usually, but rarely will you meet someone who runs a specialty nursery who can be reasonably described as *normal*, and the nurseries will usually be similarly eccentric. Some are run with military strictness, and jostling a pot out of the proper neat rows will earn you a glare of disapproval, while others are a wild jungle of seeming disorder—though invariably, the owner can put hands on precisely the plant he wants in minutes. Regardless, visiting a specialty nursery is a joy.

GROWING FROM SEED

Despite the richness of specialty nurseries, to really radically expand the range of plants you can try in your garden, you will probably want to start growing your own plants from seed. There are a multitude of reasons why growing from seed is such an excellent way to acquire new plants for your garden.

Economics

Seeds, even of rare, unusual plants, are extremely cheap. And cheap is good if you happen to be short on cash (and who isn't?), or if you have a non-gardener in your life who has that particular way of glaring at you when you come home from the nursery with a load of new specimens.

An assortment of rock garden plants ready to be shipped from Arrowhead Alpines nursery in Michigan.

Diversity

Growing from seed will also give you access to a much greater diversity of plants, not only because many species are only available as seed, but also because while ordering live plants from different countries is usually an expensive and difficult (or even impossible) process, seeds travel internationally with the greatest of ease. Many excellent seed houses will ship internationally with no fuss whatsoever, meaning you have access to a vastly larger and more interesting range of plants.

Taking chances

Seeds are often the best place to start when you want to try a plant that may or may not be adapted to your conditions. The cheapness mentioned above is nice here, because if you try and fail you aren't out a great deal of money.

But the fact that you get a whole packet of seeds makes it possible to plant many different individuals in many different locations in the garden to see where they thrive. And finally, seedlings are—sometimes a lot, sometimes a little—genetically variable, which is only a good thing. By growing out large batches of seeds, you'll be able to identify the genetically deviant individual plants that are best suited to your particular garden, and find just that precise spot on the cool north side of a stone where a gentian will thrive.

Aesthetics

You're probably skeptical about this one, but gardeners who grow from seed usually have prettier gardens than those who don't. The easiest way to make a garden look good is to plant masses and drifts of the same plant. We all know this, and yet the collector in us—when faced with a nursery or catalog full of choices—winds up buying one of everything. Bring that back to the garden, and you get a patchwork of one of this and one of that. Apparently there are people with the self-control to buy three of this and a half dozen of that, but I've never really met one of them, and I certainly could never do it (besides not being able to afford it). Seeds, however, come in big packets, and it is just as easy and cheap to sow and grow out a dozen of this and two dozen of that as it is to do just one. The very same greed and lack of self-restraint that has me buying one each of twenty different plants at the nursery works for me when I'm starting seeds, giving me attractive drifts of plants in my garden.

Seeds can be purchased from a wide range of excellent retailers, but marvelous seed exchanges are one of the great joys of rock gardening. Join any of the societies devoted to rock gardening or to specific groups or genera of plants, and you'll have access to an annual, marvelously diverse list of seeds donated by other members. And, of course, you'll also get the chance to share seeds from your favorite goodies with other gardeners from around the world.

CUTTINGS

Being comfortable propagating your plants via cuttings is wonderful. It allows you to easily turn that one impulse buy at the nursery into a more

HOW TO START ROCK GARDEN PLANTS FROM SEED

Given how wonderful and perfect starting plants from seed is, far too few gardeners do it. It is perceived as being advanced gardening, something difficult that requires a lot of work and skill to master. It really isn't, particularly starting hardy perennials like plants for a rock garden where there is no need to start the seeds indoors or use expensive light setups to get the plants growing before the weather warms up outside. There are as many ways to start seeds as there are gardeners, but this is a basic process that requires no special equipment or skills and works beautifully.

1 Start in the fall or early winter. Many seeds of winter-hardy plants require a period of cold temperatures before they'll germinate, and even those that do not won't be hurt by it. Sowing at the beginning of the cold period allows everything to germinate right on schedule come the warmer weather of spring.

2 Use seed pots. When sowing things like tomatoes or common annuals that have been bred by humans to germinate quickly and uniformly, many gardeners sow just one or two seeds directly into the small pots the seedlings will grow on in. For most plants for your rock garden, you'll be better off to sow your seeds together in a larger pot; once they've germinated, transplant the seedlings into their own individual pots. Larger pots are easier to handle, label, and they dry out less quickly. Many seeds have low and irregular germination rates, so if you sowed one seed to a pot, many of those pots would wind up empty. Sow very fine seeds directly over the surface of the soil, and cover larger seeds with soil 2–3 times their diameter.

3 Top your pots with grit. A layer of fine grit, like the gravel mulch in the rock garden, does wonders to keep seedlings healthy, particularly by keeping the bases of seedlings from succumbing to the collection of diseases known as damping off.

4 Put them outside. Leaving the pots outside over the winter gives seeds the cold treatment many species need to germinate. Come spring, being exposed to natural sunlight and wind will radically

reduce problems with damping off and produce healthy, compact seedlings that you won't have to harden off before planting out. The best place is usually against the east wall of a house or shed where they get morning sun but are protected from intense afternoon light, and where the eave can protect them from intense rainstorms. If you have a problem with rodents, cover each pot with a piece of hardware cloth to keep them from eating the seeds.

5 Prick them out. Once the seedlings have germinated in the spring and have a few true leaves, slide the soil out of the seed pot, break it up to separate the seedlings, and transplant them out into individual pots to grow on. When potting up, use the same soil mix that you use in your garden beds, which will help them root out and establish quickly once they're big enough to be placed in their final locations.

above › *Cyclamen hederifolium* seedlings in a seed pot topped with grit.

below › Dianthus seedlings pulled apart from the seed pot and ready to be transplanted into the garden.

aesthetically pleasing drift of half a dozen, to make more of a particularly vigorous or beautiful individual from a batch of diverse seedlings, or to make back-up copies of particularly fussy and beloved plants to protect against loss from hungry mammals or a cold winter. But perhaps most important, most gardeners are happy to send their friends home with a plastic baggie of cuttings if you express interest and have the wherewithal to root them.

Rooting cuttings is not technically difficult at all. For the vast majority of plants for the rock garden, you simply nip off the tip of a shoot, remove some of the lower leaves, dip it in a rooting hormone, and stick it in moist soil until it grows roots. The trick is to keep those severed stems from drying out while still giving them enough light so that they can photosynthesize to have the energy to grow roots. Luckily, most plants for the rock garden are adapted to withstand drying winds and harsh conditions and so as a group tend not to be too terribly difficult to root, though of course exceptions are numerous.

Timing is a big part of being successful with rooting cuttings. As a general rule, fresh, soft, new growth is quicker to grow roots but is also quick to dry out, while older, firmer growth resists drying out better but is slower to grow new roots. The sweet spot is somewhere in between—shoots mature enough to handle the lack of roots, but young enough to still be able to quickly grow new ones. Reference books and online resources and forums can guide you to the right timing for cuttings of many plants, and good old trial-and-error (while keeping good records so you can learn from those errors) will perfect your technique.

The equipment for rooting cuttings makes an enormous difference as well. The professional gold standard is an intermittent mist bench, where tiny nozzles regularly spray the cuttings with a fine mist of water to keep them cool and hydrated during the rooting process. This works beautifully but is not practical for most home gardeners. The best and simplest solution that I've found for the home gardener who wants to root a handful of cuttings now and again is to put moist, sterile soil (or grit or vermiculite) in a reclosable plastic bag, stick the cuttings in, and then put the bag under bright florescent lights like you would use for starting seedlings indoors. The florescent bulbs give bright light that is good for photosynthesis but produce minimal heat, so the cuttings stay cool and hydrated during the rooting process.

NURSERY BED

However you get your new plants—whether you buy them or grow them from seeds or cuttings—if you have the space, a nursery bed is a wonderful asset. In fact, I think it is a more-or-less essential part of every garden. A nursery bed is a space set aside where you can plop things that don't have a home yet: be they impulse buys at a nursery; a new plant you suspect might be a weed and don't want to set loose on a sensitive garden until you make sure; excess divisions you want to give to a friend; or seedlings, cuttings, or other new plants that need some time to grow on and bulk up before they'll look at home in a mature garden bed. If you think you don't have the space for a nursery bed, well, you probably had better find some because if you don't, all the rest of your garden will end up becoming a de facto nursery bed and everything from seedlings to new purchases will languish far too long in pots, often expiring before you make up your mind about where they go and get them in the ground.

Tracking down, acquiring, and propagating new plants is one of the great joys of gardening. It is delightful to have something cool and new in your garden to wow your friends with, and perhaps even more fun to have a few extra rooted cuttings as a gift to send them home with. As I've said many times now, rock gardens are unparalleled in giving you the maximum space to tuck in yet another marvelous new find or collection, so once you start rock gardening, be prepared to enjoy a long, long time of happily discovering, collecting, and propagating new goodies.

Plants

Cyclamen coum is typical of rock garden plants that offer both spectacular flowers and foliage.

The heart and soul of all gardening is, of course, the plants. All the beautiful rocks are just there to make the plants look good, ▶

and that perfect soil mix is just there to keep those plants growing happily. So now we finally get to dive into introducing you to the dizzyingly wide array of fascinating and beautiful plants that can be grown in the rock garden.

If you are an experienced gardener, you'll probably recognize some of the genera in the descriptions to follow, but be prepared to find them taking radically different forms than what you are used to. If you see *Gypsophila* and think of the familiar tall, airy blooms of baby's breath (*Gypsophila paniculata*), then you may be surprised by the rock-hard, centimeters-high mounds of *Gypsophila aretioides*, and few would recognize the familiar carnation (*Dianthus caryophyllus*) in the exquisite forms of alpine dianthus. Though if you look closely at the flowers, you'll probably quickly see the kinship between the alpines and their taller, looser, lowland cousins. These types of plants are exciting to me—fresh, interesting versions of a familiar plant.

You might come upon a different sort of surprise in the form of the lovely ramondas, which look for all the world like their close relatives, the African violets so familiar as houseplants. But unlike their cousins living on your windowsill, the ramondas will live happily in a shaded crevice, sailing through the coldest of winters with ease.

Beyond these plants that will be in some ways as familiar as they are new, there are also whole entirely new groups of plants which will probably not be familiar at all to the non–rock gardener, and are just waiting to blow you away with their pull-out-all-the-stops flower displays. If you've never grown a lewisia or polygala, you have a wonderful treat in store; they are some of the most beautiful plants I've ever grown, in the rock garden or anywhere else.

One of the very best things about the rock garden is that there is a seemingly endless list of plants to learn and grow. That sheer diversity means rock gardening never gets old or tired or familiar; it is forever fresh and exciting no matter how long you've been tucking plants between stones. That diversity also means that creating an exhaustive, encyclopedic listing of all the plants for a rock garden is essentially impossible. So in the section that follows, I don't attempt to tell you about every plant you could grow, but rather give you a starting point—a highly personal introduction to some of the plants for rock gardens that I think you are going to enjoy getting to know and growing. I've tried to focus on some of the easier-to-grow options for beginners, ranging from the classic mainstays of rock gardening like saxifrages, dianthus, and lewisias to less traditional varieties like miniature hostas for the shaded rock garden, as well as some plants that I just personally love too much to not include, like the bewitching blooms of *Echinocereus* cactus.

Cacti

Though not traditional inhabitants of the rock garden, cacti are perfectly suited to most of them, with their sculptural forms and over-the-top floral displays. Dry desert lands, like high alpine regions, have a low concentration of pollinating insects and other animals, so many cacti, like alpines, have evolved massive, brightly colored flowers in order to ensure that the pollinators do find their blooms. Like alpines they require excellent drainage, especially to ensure maximal hardiness, and so will be happy in the loose, open soil of the rock garden. Unlike true alpines, however, cacti as a group thrive in hot weather, and so are good alternatives for gardeners in warmer climates where most truly high-altitude plants will shrivel and die.

Cactus is a family, Cactaceae, comprising over a hundred genera and over a thousand species native to the Americas. The deserts of Africa, Asia, and Australia are the home of similar but unrelated succulent plants; unfortunately non-native cacti, especially opuntias, have naturalized aggressively in many dry climates around the world.

The long white spines of *Cylindropuntia echinocarpa* are as pleasing to the eye as they are painful to the touch.

The most obvious appeal of a cactus is its form. Totally unlike other plants, their sculptural shapes are a wonderful contrast to the rest of the garden. The prickly spines of cactus are also a great part of their visual appeal, like the brutally sharp but very beautiful long, bright-white spines of *Cylindropuntia echinocarpa*. That vicious armament of course must be treated with respect, and when working around cactus, move slowly and watch what you are doing. I usually get stabbed when I notice a weed and instinctively reach to pull it out before my brain catches up to tell me I'm doing something stupid. Far worse than the long, easily visible spines, however, are the glochids found on some species, especially in the genus *Opuntia*. Glochids are tiny hairs, barely even visible, armed with minuscule backward-facing barbs that lodge irritatingly and seemingly irremovably in your skin. If you do get glochid-ed, the best way to get them out is either to put a piece of strong tape, like duct tape, or a layer of rubber cement over the area, then rip the tape or dried rubber cement off. Yes, both approaches might take some hair with them, which is why thick gloves and great care are better options for working with cactus.

Opuntia fragilis 'Lake of the Woods' is tiny enough for even the smallest rock garden or trough.

Luckily, cacti in the garden are extremely low maintenance, so once you have them in the ground you should rarely need to fuss with them or put yourself in range of their bad temper. Given their extreme drought tolerance, cacti beds are usually too dry for the standard garden weeds; if you do get weeds in your cactus bed, it is well worth knowing that the thick skin of almost all cacti will not absorb the herbicide glyphosate, so you can spray over them and kill the weeds without harming the cacti in the slightest. If you don't use herbicides in the garden, invest in a pair of thick gloves and a long, sturdy set of forceps to extract weeds from between the spiny pads.

The added benefit of those spines is that they make cacti one of the few really, truly, absolutely all the time deer- and rabbit-proof plants. And human-proof as well—I will confess that when I found out the neighborhood children at my previous garden were in the habit of riding their

The flowers of *Echinocereus coccineus*, seen here at the J C Raulston Arboretum in North Carolina, can hardly be beat.

bicycles off the sidewalk and through my lawns and beds, I seriously considered a little cactus border to keep them in check. It would have worked, I think, though it might have also gotten me sued.

Spines and sculptural forms are not all cactus have to offer; their flowers are almost without exception large, brilliantly colored, and very beautiful—the better to attract the sparse pollinators in desert regions. A prime example of this are the rich-red cups of *Echinocereus coccineus*. However, before you purchase a cactus based on its floral display, be aware that those huge flowers are often extremely short-lived, usually lasting a matter of days or even only a few hours. But what a display when it is going on! There is a certain appeal to their incredible brevity—it makes the flowering of a cactus a dramatic event, one worth anticipating and taking off early from work or staying up late (depending on when they bloom) to enjoy, but do be aware that most of the time the aesthetic impact they bring to your garden will be based on their form and spines, not the oh-so-brief flowering.

When most people think of cactus they think of warm climates, and of course the greatest diversity of this family is indeed native to hot deserts, but many of them are perfectly suitable for areas with cold winters as well. The genus *Opuntia*, the iconic prickly pears with the classic flat pads, has native ranges that stretch up into frigid Canada. Many of the western American species, especially the beautiful genus *Echinocereus*, have ranges that extend far up into the extremely cold heights of the Rocky Mountains, so while gardeners with mild winters have the widest range of options, cold climate gardeners needn't be left out.

The key to growing cactus is drainage, especially in cool weather when they are not in active growth. Cacti in general will respond to regular watering with enthusiastic growth during warm, sunny weather, but once they go dormant in the winter, soggy conditions are the kiss of death. In fact, for gardeners like myself trying to grow hardy cacti in a wet, northerly climate, water is a far bigger issue than cold. I've seen many a hardy cactus or succulent come through intense cold just fine, only to rot out and die in the prolonged sog of early spring. So put cacti in a spot with the sharpest drainage; and for the fussiest species, they're probably best grown in containers that can be moved under a sheltering eave or unheated shed to keep all rainfall off of them in cold weather.

One interesting way to grow the cacti that demand perfect drainage in wet climates is to graft them. Fussy but beautiful species can be grafted onto the roots of more robust and adaptable varieties to get a more reliable specimen. Choose the toughest, easiest-to-grow cactus in your area as a rootstock; for most of us, that will be an opuntia. Slice the rootstock off near the base, and then slice off the top of the scion that you will be grafting on top. The two pieces should be roughly the same size, though it isn't critical. Look at your cut surfaces and find the vascular rings, which will look a little like the core of a carrot, a ring of lighter colored tissue. Place the scion on the rootstock so their vascular rings overlap and hold it in firmly in place—a rubber band stretched over the whole plant works well. Set the grafted plant in a warm, humid place for about a week while the graft union forms, and your graft is good to go.

Opuntia, the prickly pears, are probably the most frequently seen hardy cactus in the north, often *Opuntia polyacantha*, which has classic cactus pads and huge yellow (or pink, or orange, in some forms) flowers in early summer. Though I rarely see it for sale, it usually isn't hard to acquire from a friend, as pads pulled off (with tongs or very thick gloves) and simply dropped in a good spot will root and grow almost effortlessly. Less commonly seen is *Opuntia fragilis* 'Lake of the Woods'. *Opuntia fragilis* is a wide-ranging, diverse species, and 'Lake of the Woods' is named for the park in Canada where this cultivar was originally found, making it one of the most northerly cacti in the world. Extreme cold tolerance is one great reason to grow this selection, but it has much else to recommend it as well. The pads are the smallest of any *Opuntia* specimen I have seen; each one is about the size of a quarter or the last segment of my index finger, making an extremely cute little mound that is perfectly in scale with the smallest of rock garden plants and adorable in a trough or other container. One of my favorite things about this selection is that despite having long, very sharp spines, it does not have any, or at least has very few, glochids. Bump into it, and you'll say ouch, but you won't spend the next hour trying to pick tiny, vicious hairs out of your skin.

Opuntia humifusa is common and widely adaptable, but no less beautiful for all that.

Less common and harder to track down than the opuntias, but very beautiful and well worth growing, are various species from the genus *Echinocereus*. Many species are hardy to at least USDA zone 5 if kept dry, and boast some truly lovely plants—from the rich red flowers of *E. coccineus* and *E. triglochidiatus*, to the brilliant yellows of *Echinocereus dasyacanthus*. It is a ridiculously beautiful genus, with relatively long-lasting flowers and some really great colors of spines. Add in a blessed lack of irritating glochids, and I think they're the perfect genus of cactus for most rock gardens. You should be aware that many, if not most, species of *Echinocereus* are extremely variable in the wild; depending on where seeds were originally collected, the same species can show a wide range of different colored flowers and spines, and quite a bit of variation in winter hardiness. Taking the time to inquire about the plant's provenance is often a good idea, particularly if you are trying to grow them in a cold climate and want the most northerly, highest altitude forms of the species.

Campanulas

At first blush, many campanulas are pretty similar. Virtually every member of this massive genus has small, bell-shaped, purpley blue flowers. There are white forms of many species and the very occasional pink, but other than that, it is all lavender blue, all the time. Some species have more open, spreading, star-shaped flowers, but on the whole, campanula flowers are pretty much the same. If this sounds like a bad thing, it isn't. That standard campanula flower is quite lovely, and what they lack in diversity of flower form and color, they make up for with an incredible range of growth habits, bloom times, and architecture.

In a genus this large, there are a few black sheep that have given the rest of the group a bad name, particularly the ones that like to run—such as *Campanula punctata*—which have made an attempt to conquer by force every garden they were ever planted in. Don't let those obnoxious brutes ruin your appreciation of the choice rock garden species that are quite beautiful and well behaved. Even the dwarf species that do run, like

Campanula carpatica 'Blue Clips' may be thought of as common, but it's a proven performer.

Campanula cochlearifolia tends to ramble through the rock garden, looking wonderful wherever it ends up.

C. cochlearifolia, do so with restraint and are so small they'll never smother anything.

One thing I really like about campanulas in the rock garden is that while being supremely adapted to the dry conditions—many of them being the ultimate plants for growing in rock walls—they don't look that way. Rather than the tight mounds of small, dense, often glaucous leaves that so many alpines form, the alpine campanulas, though small, still have larger, looser, bright green leaves. Not that I don't love tight, dense mounds of glaucous leaves, but a whole garden of them can be a bit much, and the look of a campanula in the mix is a delightful contrast.

That loose, greener look to campanulas is a clue to their culture, in that with very few exceptions, the alpine campanulas like a bit of shade. Not a lot, but some shelter from the afternoon sun will be appreciated in almost all climates, and they are typically better suited to the east side of a bank or wall than the south. You'll know when you've got them in the right spot, as they tend to self-sow moderately when happy, which is of course the perfect way to let them colonize a stone wall.

Of the many wonderful species for the rock garden, one of the best is *Campanula portenschlagiana*. This is the iconic rock garden campanula, and you have probably seen pictures of it seeding around into the crevices of stone walls, where it thrives and looks absolutely amazing. This species, when happy, is very hard to beat in terms of floral display. Plants are small, less then 6 inches tall and wide, and when they flower in the spring they

Campanula portenschlagiana blooming vigorously in cracks between paving stones.

go all-out, producing flowering stems up to 8 inches long, so loaded with small, blue, star-shaped flowers that they all but obscure the rest of the plant. The flowering stems like to trail gracefully, and so are marvelous on the edge of a raised bed or container, or planted in a stone wall where they can weep down dramatically. There are several named cultivars available, one of best being 'Resholdt's Variety'.

Among the very tiniest is *Campanula cochlearifolia*, with an extremely high cuteness factor. This species creeps along at mere centimeters high, and produces tiny, delicate blue, bell-shaped flowers in the spring, only an inch or two long dancing on delicate stems up above the low foliage. *Campanula cochlearifolia* is a runner, but spreads more by migrating, dying out in one spot to pop up somewhere new. In the garden they seem to wind up against the edge of a rock, or, when grown in a container, at the edge of a pot. I'm not sure if this is just chance, that the running rhizomes stop when they hit a stone or pot edge, or if there is some active adaptation that sends them there—perhaps the coolness of the rock, or the chance to catch dewy runoff? But whatever the reason, creeping along the edge of something seems to be where they are the happiest, which is nice because that is really where this species looks best. As tiny and as delicate as it is, it is easily lost in the middle of a garden. I really think it's best suited to a trough or other container garden to save you having to get down on your knees to enjoy the delicate flowers.

Probably the most widely available of the dwarf campanulas is *C. carpatica*, and cultivars like 'Blue Clips' and similar selections pop up in garden centers because they look very cute in a pot, flower heavily, and are quick and easy for nurseries to produce. Plants are a few inches tall, and bloom with almost ridiculously large blue or white flowers sitting right on top of the foliage. Don't let their commonness blind you to this species' very good attributes, as the floral display really is top notch, and most selections will re-bloom heavily throughout the summer. Be aware, however, that this isn't a long-lived species, tending to bloom itself to death after a few years. You can either plan on replacing them periodically, or better yet, use them as temporary fillers for blank spaces around things like dwarf conifers and daphnes, which will expand over the years to take up the space vacated by *C. carpatica*.

Conifers

Use caution when dipping your toes into the wide and wonderful world of tiny conifers. It is an easy slide down the slippery slope from putting in a couple of inexpensive miniature chamaecyparis to becoming a full-on "cone head" obsessively collecting ever more and more tiny conifers and even indulging in witch hunts.

The term "cone head" is fairly obvious: conifers produce cones, and conifer freaks are addicted to them. Witch hunting requires a little more explanation. Most conifers, the familiar pines, spruces, firs, and so forth, grow into large trees, but for whatever reason are prone to chance mutations that result in small, tight, congested growth. When these chance mutations occur on a branch of a large tree, the result is a normal-looking tree with a strange ball of miniaturized branches in the middle of it. That lump of tight, congested growth is called a witches' broom, and they are where most new varieties of small conifers come

from. Cone heads go out witch hunting, looking for witches' brooms usually in winter when there is (a) nothing else to do in the garden and (b) no leaves on the deciduous trees to obscure the witches' brooms on the conifers. Once they find a broom, they take a few pieces (by climbing up to it, or sometimes more dramatically by shooting down parts of the broom with a gun), graft them onto a normal rootstock to propagate it, and give their new dwarf form a name. Most witches' brooms don't produce cones and so are more or less sterile. But sometimes there is one that will cone, and from those seed can be collected, which will result in a whole series of different seedlings with varying degrees of dwarfing.

But fertile brooms producing dwarf seedlings are unusual; the majority of dwarf conifers originate by chance, found by sharp-eyed enthusiasts. That makes the world of dwarf conifers rather different from that of most other groups of plants. For most plants, new varieties are created by breeders

far left › **Where dwarf conifers come from: a witches' broom on a spruce, lifted and growing all together at Hidden Lake Gardens in Michigan.**

left › *Pinus contorta* var. *latifolia* 'Chief Joseph' has **exceptional winter color, but needs to be sheltered—as it is here—from winter sun to prevent burning.**

carefully cross-pollinating, harvesting seeds, and selecting plants that meet their preconceived goals. New dwarf conifers arise by chance, so there is no way to create a really lovely dwarf blue fir, for example, other than to hike through large populations and hope you find a broom. Witches' brooms are rare enough to be very exciting to find out in the wild but common enough that if you are looking for them, you can frequently find them. I've personally found two, one on a Scots pine and one on a Norway spruce, just riding through urban neighborhoods on a bicycle. That sort of rare-but-not-really reality of brooms means that when people find them they often want to propagate and name them, because, well, it is a new broom! How cool! But those new brooms are often not particularly distinct or better than existing dwarf varieties, resulting in long, long, *long* lists of varieties available to collectors in specialty nurseries, many of which are only marginally different in growth habit. This can make it a little overwhelming for the beginner, but also means that you can usually find precisely the traits you are looking for if you keep searching long enough.

Not all dwarf conifers originate as witches' brooms. Junipers, in particular, are highly variable in growth habit, and new forms can be found

Abies koreana 'Kahouts Icebreaker' is small and tight, with stunning white recurved needles.

through traditional selection from seedlings or searching out particularly small forms in the wild. Mugo pines and a few other conifers also produce individual seedlings that are dwarf to varying degrees, while some of the witches' brooms do cone and so new forms can be bred from them in the traditional way.

Dwarf conifers bring a lot to the rock garden. Aesthetically, they provide much-needed height where sometimes all the little flat buns of plants can begin to look all the same. Perhaps even more important, especially in climates with a long, cold winter, conifers are invaluable because they look great 365 days a year, in stark contrast to the much briefer displays of herbaceous perennials or deciduous shrubs. Loving conifers is about embracing a diversity of form and texture, and reveling in the many marvelous shades of green—from the dark, glossy tones of Japanese umbrella pine to the blues of concolor fir and Colorado blue spruce, to the bright yellow-green of some chamaecyparis and the many yellow-needled pine selections.

Microbiota decussata is usually a flat groundcover, but here is grafted onto a standard to form a small tree.

Despite their year-round reliability, conifers offer a lot of seasonal variation in their beauty and appearance. Needle color changes dramatically in winter for some conifers. The brightest of the yellow-needled pines, varieties like 'Chief Joseph', for example, are a brilliant school bus–yellow in the winter, fading through chartreuse to dull green with the arrival of warmer temperatures. On virtually all conifers the new shoots in spring—called candles for some reason—emerge in bright, vibrant shades that contrast beautifully with the duller tones of the mature needles. And many, despite being evergreens, have great fall color. Though the needles last over the winter, each individual needle only lives a year or two, and the old needles get shed in the fall. Though they'll never rival the colors of a sugar maple, needles often turn a nice shade of yellow before falling, which can make a lovely contrast with the newer needles that are still green and ready to head into winter. The effect is

A rich collection of dwarf conifers makes up the bulk of Paula Flynn's Iowa rock garden.

particularly nice on white pine selections, as long as you don't freak out and think your pine is dying, as novice gardeners often, and understandably, do.

Culture of conifers is simple. In general, they don't like wet feet and prefer a well-drained soil, but beyond that are not very demanding. It is also well worth remembering that dwarf conifers are usually less tolerant of drought then their full-sized equivalents. When the top half of the plant is dwarf, the bottom half—the roots—are dwarf as well, so shallower root systems can't delve as deep for water, making them not well suited for extremely dry, harsh locations.

Many catalogs and references will list mature sizes for dwarf conifer varieties, but it is important to know that even a very tiny dwarf conifer never stops growing. Well, at least not until it dies, which hopefully won't happen to yours for a very, very long time. Instead, in good conditions they'll put on a fairly consistent amount of new growth annually, ranging from less than an inch a year (what is classified as a miniature form by the American Conifer Society) to about 6 inches a year for the larger dwarf

A sampling of *Picea pungens,* from large to small, in Brigitta Stewart's Michigan garden.

varieties. So you need to think not about what the mature size is, but about how big the plant will be in 5 years, in 10 years, and so forth. Good reference works and nurseries will be able to tell you the annual growth rate of a variety, and the American Conifer Society has a massive database of conifer varieties along with growth rates (and a lot of other information) on their website. But if you are looking at a plant in person, you can easily tell just by looking. If you look at a branch, there is a distinct node, and usually secondary branches, separating each year's growth. Just measure that segment of annual growth—or, even better, measure the growth from the past several years and average them—to get an idea of how fast the plant will grow in your garden.

If a conifer is going to outgrow the space you've got for it, you can slow it down by pruning. The best way to do this is by "candling," pinching back each shoot of the soft, new growth in the spring to half or three-quarters of its original size. This will very effectively slow down the growth of the plant, but of course it only takes a couple of busy springs (and what gardener ever had a spring that wasn't busy?) for a shrub to get away from you.

The best practice is to plant your conifers nice and far apart, then inter-plant them with other things that you can sacrifice or transplant as the conifers get bigger. Perennials obviously work well, as does alternating the choicest, most expensive conifers with cheaper, more expendable options like junipers and chamaecyparis.

Conifers can be pricey, and some radically more so than others. In terms of pricing, there are two main groups of conifers: those that can be propagated by cuttings (junipers, thujas, chamaecyparis) and those that are grafted (pines, spruce, firs). Rooting cuttings is cheap, easy, and low-tech; grafting is a skill that takes time, a bit of talent to acquire and special conditions to pull off, and pricing reflects those differences in propagation. Oddly, sometimes we also let that price difference influence how we think about the plants. Junipers, in particular, never seem to get quite the love they deserve simply because they are cheap and very easy to grow, even though they can also be every bit as lovely as a much, much pricier dwarf spruce or fir.

But regardless, a nice dwarf conifer can be quite an investment for your rock garden—and an excellent one at that; it will only get lovelier with age. With this in mind, it is important to choose the right variety for your garden and conditions, and there really are some very bad choices to be made, depending on where you are. Where I garden in Michigan, Colorado blue spruce (*Picea pungens* 'Glauca') is beautiful, popular, and a terrible plant. The local agriculture university has a plant diagnostic center where people can send sick plant samples to get the problem diagnosed, and a technician there told me that they see more samples of blue spruces than anything else, by a mile. They diligently diagnose the problem, and tell the owner of the sick tree that they can treat the various problems with various chemicals, but their real advice is to cut it down and plant something better. Take a tree native to the dry, thin air of the Rocky Mountains, and put it in the wet, humid climate of Michigan, and basically all hell breaks loose.

To avoid problems like that, and to get a good sense of what your plants will look like as they mature in your garden, the very best way to find good conifers for your garden is to visit local botanic gardens or arboretums. See what looks good there and what really strikes your eye, as the full beauty of these plants simply isn't apparent from a small graft sitting in a nursery pot.

Cyclamen

Not true alpines by any stretch of the imagination, hardy cyclamen are essential for the shady rock garden. Okay, so I happen to think that they are essential for any garden. I'm something of a cyclamen nut, and have been for a while. I grew my first *Cyclamen coum* when I was in my teens, and enthused so loudly and constantly about how in love with them I was that my older brother made me a shirt for Christmas that said simply "*Cyclamen coum*" on the front. I still wear it with pride, though to be honest, I'm more of a *C. hederifolium* man these days.

Cyclamen is a big genus, but there are three species that are the hardiest and most widely adaptable, with the most available forms and variations: *Cyclamen coum*, *C. hederifolium*, and *C. purpurascens*. Let me state explicitly that one cyclamen I am not talking about here is *C. persicum*, the florist cyclamen. Though lovely, it is tender and in most cases has been bred to be so large, lush, and exuberant that even where hardy it would look rather out of place in most rock gardens.

Cyclamen hederifolium 'Amaze Me White' has an ethereal loveliness.

All the cyclamens are geophytes; they get called a bulb, though they're technically a tuber. Each seedling forms one tuber—a flattened roundish disk—which unlike a true bulb doesn't divide; instead it simply gets larger and larger each year. After 15 years or so happy plants can easily be as big as a dinner plate. It is possible to propagate mature tubers by slicing them in half or smaller pieces, but that isn't particularly reliable, as the cut surfaces are prone to rotting. Almost without exception, therefore, cyclamen are propagated by seed. Tissue culture protocol has been worked out, and at least one United States company was releasing tissue cultured *C. coum* varieties, but last I knew had stopped production because there wasn't sufficient demand. Sadly, it is still very common for commercially available cyclamen, especially very cheap ones sold alongside tulips and daffodils, to be wild-collected—a deplorable practice that is doing real and significant damage to natural populations of these beautiful plants.

Another way in which cyclamen differ from other "bulbs" is that even when dormant, they don't like drying out completely. A dormant tulip or daffodil can by dried out to almost nothing, and will then happily come back into growth once it gets into the ground. Do the same to a dormant cyclamen, and it will usually never do anything at all. The tuber will still look perfectly firm and sound, often sitting for years looking absolutely fine, but will never break growth. When I give talks and mention hardy cyclamen in the States, invariably someone will raise a hand and say they didn't turn out to be truly hardy. Which is when I ask them where they got them, and equally invariably, it was from a big bulb company alongside an order of tulips and daffodils. These cyclamen are quite easy to grow. It just helps to start with a plant that is actually alive. If possible, get your cyclamen from a nursery that you know propagates them (rather than destroying wild populations), and in active growth in a pot.

Hardy cyclamen are incredibly adaptable plants. For species that are dormant in the summer (*C. coum* and *C. hederifolium*), you want to place them somewhere they'll be on the dry side in the summer. This usually is not hard to do, even in a wet summer climate area; planting them among deciduous trees works beautifully. They perform best in light shade, and will grow in deeper shade, though flowering will be reduced.

Cyclamen suffer from few problems, aside from small, evil, furry

Some of the bewildering diversity of foliage patterns available from *Cyclamen hederifolium*.

mammals. Cyclamen tubers are apparently delicious, and mice, voles, and squirrels can devour them with gusto. The usual practices of either planting the tubers in a wire cage or using repellents, traps, or a not overfed cat, can keep the rodent spawn of the devil at bay. Other than that, cyclamen are carefree and easy.

Most of the hardy cyclamen are in active growth during the winter, with leaves emerging in late summer to late winter and then vanishing sometime in the early summer. I used to think this lack of foliage in the summer was a disadvantage, but I've totally come around to a different point of view. True, a bed of nothing but *C. hederifolium* will be awfully barren at midsummer, but combine them in the shady rock garden with a typical winter-dormant perennial like a miniature hosta and you've got a match made in heaven. When the hostas go down, up come the cyclamen; and when the cyclamen are fading, up come the hostas to replace them. The other great thing about

summer-dormant cyclamen is that not being in active growth makes them incredibly tolerant of summer drought and difficult dry shade conditions, and so perfect for a dry, shady rock garden.

Flowers of the hardy cyclamen are lovely and have that uniquely cyclamen swept back look. For all three species, flower color varies from the typical magenta to white shades, to bicolors that are white or pale pink with dark magenta at the base of the flower. Many boast a ravishing fragrance. Unlike the florist cyclamen, which have been bred extensively for flower size and color, there aren't particularly dramatic floral selections in hardy cyclamen, at least not yet.

Foliage, in contrast, has been an area of great interest for hardy cyclamen breeding, and quite honestly I think their foliage far, far outshines the flowers. All the cyclamen in their wild forms have dark-green leaves patterned to some degree with silver markings. Selective breeding for the hardy garden cyclamen has focused much more on leaves than flowers, and the result is a wide range of beautiful patterned leaf forms, including usually the most popular form, a brilliant solid silver which glows in a shade garden. Given that cyclamen are propagated by seed, not asexually, these leaf patterns come in the form of different seed strains, which are usually somewhat variable. So if possible, buy your cyclamen in leaf, in person, so you can pick out the particular individuals with the leaves you like the best.

Cyclamen coum is often the first hardy cyclamen people go for, because it flowers at that most desirable time of year—late winter to insanely early spring alongside other brave flowers like galanthus and eranthis. Flowers range from magenta to white, and have distinctively short, stubby, rounded petals. Leaves emerge from summer dormancy in late summer or early winter, and are round. Only a few color patterns are available: the wild-type green with silver spots, silver leaf forms which have just a thin green edge, and the ever popular "Christmas tree" forms with a Christmas tree–shaped green center surrounded by bright silver. As nice as they are, this is my least favorite of the hardy cyclamen because they lack fragrance in the flowers, have little diversity of leaf patterns, and, for me anyway, are the least robust and vigorous of the hardy cyclamen.

Cyclamen hederifolium is my favorite species, hands down. Flowers come up in the late summer just before the foliage, and I adore their fresh

above › *Cyclamen hederifolium* leaves against rocks in Dan Heims's garden in Portland, Oregon.

below › *Cyclamen coum* 'Something Magic', a lovely "Christmas tree" selection.

burst of pink or (my favorite) white flowers, which have long, elegant petals and are fragrant in some forms. *Cyclamen hederifolium* also seems to be the most vigorous of the hardy cyclamen; they grow beautifully for me here in Michigan, as well as chilly Minnesota; Helsinki, Finland; and even sweltering South Carolina. The best part of this species, however, is the insane diversity of leaf forms. Color can range from absolutely solid silver with not a speck of green to almost solid green with a dizzying array of intricately patterned green and silver forms in between that are my favorites. And the shape of the leaf is endlessly variable as well, ranging from the classic ivy-shaped ones to long, narrow, arrowhead shapes, smooth leaf edges to jagged ones, and even ones with a slightly frilled or wavy leaf margin.

In my book, *Cyclamen purpurascens* is a close runner-up for favorite after *C. hederifolium*, and gardeners in Minnesota and Colorado report that for them, it is the most vigorous of the hardy species. *Cyclamen purpurascens* has a couple things going for it. Unlike the other hardy species, it does not go dormant in the summer, meaning you can enjoy the lovely foliage year-round, although this also means it is far less tolerant of summer drought and dry shade conditions. The leaves are round and range in color from green to silver with a few different patterns in between, more diverse than *C. coum* but not coming close to the diversity of *C. hederifolium*. Flowering starts in the summer and continues on into the fall to overlap with the beginning of the *C. hederifolium* bloom, and one of the very best things about this species is the incredible strong, delicious fragrance of the flowers.

Whichever species you try, add some cyclamen to the garden. You won't regret it.

Late winter or early spring flowers of *Cyclamen coum.*

Daphnes

The name daphne comes from Greek myths, a girl so lovely that Apollo "fell in love" with her and started chasing her, presumably to rape her. Because, you know, that is what Greek gods did to girls they "fell in love" with. Daphne quite reasonably objected to this, and so called out to her father, another god, who cleverly turned her into a shrub (though oddly she was turned into a bay laurel, not this shrub that bears her name). Good going, Dad. Yes, you stopped the rape. The bad news, your daughter now photosynthesizes.

Befitting their namesake, daphnes are spectacularly beautiful shrubs. They also have a reputation for being finicky and difficult to grow. But really, if I'd been almost raped and then turned into a shrub, I'd not be just finicky—I'd be equal parts furious and terrified. So give the daphnes some slack. Daphnes, in fact, aren't all that difficult, they are just a little particular about the conditions they grow in, but give them the right soil conditions and they're really quite tough and easy.

If you live in a warm climate, especially the southern United States, the daphne you know will probably be *Daphne odora*, which is insanely, spectacularly, dizzyingly fragrant, but a bit large for a rock garden. It hails from China along with some of the other warm climate daphnes, and they are quite unlike the alpine species. They want wetter, more organic soil, and even perhaps a little shade.

The rock garden daphnes are a different beast altogether. Here we're talking about shrubs that hail mostly from the Caucasus Mountains in eastern Europe, a continental climate with hot summers, cold winters, and dry, rocky, well-drained soil. And that soil is what they need in the garden. Daphnes have a reputation for just up and dying due to root rots. That is easily preventable, even in rainy climates, by planting them in rock garden conditions where they have perfect drainage. Give them the right soil and daphnes are easy, long-lived, and carefree. The only other thing to remember is that daphnes do not like having their roots disturbed. Forget moving mature plants in your garden, and my personal experience—backed up by numerous other people—is that large daphnes in pots rarely transplant well. You are much better off buying a small plant, recently rooted cuttings, or seedlings. That can be a hard sell, because daphnes are terrible nursery plants, relatively expensive to produce; it can be a bit of a leap to pay top price for a tiny little plant, but that's what will do best in your garden. And it is worth it. Those tiny plants bulk up surprisingly fast once you get them in ground.

Since daphnes do transplant poorly except when tiny, if you are going to put them in a trough or other container make sure the plant is small enough and the trough large enough so that they can stay there. This is not a plant you can pop out of the trough and graduate to the open garden once it gets big.

All the small alpine-type daphnes I talk about here have been absolutely, without a doubt, totally hardy for over 20 years in Michigan, USDA zone 5, and thrive for friends in the sometimes even more extreme climate of Iowa. But some of them will fail to overwinter in the much milder weather of winter in the United Kingdom. It seems that these daphnes do best where it is very cold and they stay frozen all winter, warming up to hot quickly in the spring and summer and spending little time in the cool,

above › Daphne petraea in bloom.

below › The subtly variegated beauty of Daphne 'Stasek'.

wet conditions that can cause them to rot off. So if you live in a continental climate with cold winters and hot summers and have cursed all the plants you can't seem to grow, this is the group for you! They'll thrive in a way they never do in milder places.

In the United States the most common of the daphnes (excepting *Daphne odora* in the South) is *D. ×burkwoodii* 'Carol Mackie'. Carol is a nice enough shrub—maturing to a roughly three-foot sphere, leaves with a narrow variegated edge, and bunches of small pinky white, somewhat fragrant flowers in the spring. She's lovely. All daphnes are. She's also just about the worst daphne out there. Carol, and the other *×burkwoodii* cultivars, all have a terrible habit of splitting open at the base once they mature. This usually doesn't harm the plant, but instead of a tidy, attractive shrub, you suddenly have a giant, sprawly mess. The one *×burkwoodii* variety well worth growing is 'Briggs Moonlight', which has insanely beautiful yellow-white leaves outlined with the smallest edge of green. One of the most striking variegated plants out there, it also has so little chlorophyll that it is very slow growing, fussy, and difficult to propagate. But in general, you're better off going for some of the smaller, evergreen, alpine options.

Even out of flower, *Daphne* 'Lawrence Crocker' is a lovely thing every day of the year.

The graceful beauty of the Delphi form of *Daphne jasminea* creeping over a hunk of tufa.

One of the best—and easiest to grow—of these is 'Lawrence Crocker', a terrific shrub only 6 to 8 inches tall but eventually getting quite wide. Brigitta Stewart's nearly 20-year-old plant in Michigan is a good three feet across now. It's one of the most carefree of daphnes (if you are going to put one in a less-than-ideal spot, this is the one to go with). Terrific evergreen foliage that always looks great, and one of the really top-notch spring flowering displays, sometimes totally covering the leaves with a thick layer of fragrant purple flowers. The spring bloom is off the charts, and it usually follows up with a nice re-bloom once or twice in the summer, not as nice as the spring one, but still a very welcome bonus.

If Lawrence is still too large for you, try smaller species like *Daphne cneorum*, *D. petraea*, and *D. juliae*. These three species are the elite of the very small rock garden daphnes, especially and most dramatically *D. petraea*, which makes the tiniest, densest, most incredibly flower-laden plant,

and is also a bit notorious. Difficult to root from cuttings (mostly because it grows so slowly it produces little in the way of cutting material), slow to grow on in a nursery, and unhappy in all but the most perfect garden conditions. Not a plant for a beginner. *Daphne cneorum* and *D. juliae* are similar plants for lesser mortals; not quite as small, though they too can pull off the so-many-flowers-you-can't-see-the-leaves trick, and *D. cneorum* will give you that heavy bloom two or three times a year.

Generally less fussy and every bit as nice as these species are various hybrid forms. *Daphne ×hendersonii,* which occurs naturally in the wild and has been recreated many times by humans, most notably by daphne breeding god Robin White, is a hybrid swarm that is my favorite of the really small daphnes for rock gardens. The hybrid vigor makes these easier to grow than the elite species I talk about above. They root fairly easily and make decent plants in the nursery, and will usually repeat bloom at least twice more over the course of the summer. Fragrance is nice, and flower colors range from dark pink to white. Other hybrids, like the lightly variegated 'Stasek', are wonderful as well.

And then tiniest of all and one of my very favorites is *Daphne jasminea*. This species is in a class by itself, the smallest of the small. Very unlike the other rock garden daphnes, which tend to form a tight, dense mound of foliage, *D. jasminea* thinks it is a bonsai. That is just how it grows, no pruning required. It stays tiny, but quickly develops an impressively thick, gnarled trunk and branches, while the blue-green leaves are thin enough that you can easily see and appreciate the beautiful form. Flowering is never heavy, but the light scattering of highly fragrant white blooms is constant—pick a day, any day, from spring to late summer, and *D. jasminea* will be in flower. There are two forms commonly in cultivation, neither of which has a proper cultivar name, generally just being called the upright form, which, as you can guess grows upright to form a small rounded bush only 3 or 4 inches tall, and the Delphi or creeping form, which, you got it, creeps. The Delphi form is my favorite. Plant it against a really nice rock and it will form itself into a magnificent sculpture, turning in just 5 or 6 years into something that wouldn't look out of place in a collection of 100-year-old bonsai. This is certainly the best species for a trough or container. It stays tiny so it won't outgrow the space, and this really is something you'll want to have up close where you can appreciate it.

left › *Daphne cneorum* blooming its head off once again, in October, at the Denver Botanic Gardens.

below › *Daphne ×burkwoodii* 'Briggs Moonlight' is one of the most strongly variegated plants out there. Brilliant, beautiful, and fussy as can be.

Dianthus

Dianthus is a massive genus with a huge range, from the classic sweet William of cottage gardens to florist's carnations. But it is in the rock garden that dianthus shine, with numerous species that form beautiful, tight mounds and buns, absolute rock garden classics along with taller—but still perfectly appropriate for the rock garden—species and forms. Foliage is very nice, often a bright glaucous blue and evergreen; the floral display is almost always breathtaking. Dianthus flowers range in color from white through pink to dark magenta (though there are a few weak yellows here and there), but that limited range of color is made up for by often having intricately and uniquely patterned blooms, like those found in many forms of *Dianthus alpinus*. Double forms abound and petals can range from having a merely jagged "pinked" edge to a dramatic fringe trailing long threads, like those of *Dianthus superbus*, and the flowers are often elaborately patterned with spots and bands of contrasting colors. On top of the great visual diversity of the flowers, most

The intricately patterned blooms of *Dianthus alpinus*.

species also boast wonderful fragrance, often a bright, spicy tone reminiscent of cloves.

As a group dianthus like good drainage, and as a rule of thumb, the smaller and tighter the plant and the bluer the foliage, the pickier they are about that drainage. For the very tight buns, good drainage at the soil surface is especially critical as the tight growth holds moisture, making them prone to rot out in rainy, humid climates. Oddly, and in my experience pretty much unique to dianthus, when basal rot does set in, it often does not kill the entire plant, just one chunk or section of the bun. This can leave the plants looking odd and patchy at first, but they'll grow back in. When I see a section of the plant turning brown, usually in the sog of spring, I'll pre-emptively cut it out. That helps keep the rot from spreading, and opening up the bun a little allows the rest of the plant to dry out, preventing new sections of rot from starting. This tendency to rot out is particularly

left › *Dianthus superbus* flowers are both deeply scented and very odd in a way that you will either love or hate.

above › **Self-sown masses of mongrel dianthus put on a show in Brigitta Stewart's rock garden at Arrowhead Alpines in Michigan.**

pronounced in hot, humid areas like the American Southeast, and dianthus are not generally a good choice for those climates.

Self-sowing is the norm for happy dianthus, which can be a problem or a boon depending on your point of view. I rather like it: I'm not much for strict control in the garden and if I'm going to have weeds (which, let's face it, I am) I'd rather they be something pretty. Many species and varieties will interbreed as well, which I also rather like, producing clouds of variable plants that blend together nicely. If you dislike the self-seeding, deadheading is the obvious and easy solution, with the added bonus of encouraging the occasional late summer re-bloom. However, it is worth leaving a few plants to go to seed; though the tight, bun-forming species can be extremely long-lived, the taller ones tend to have shorter lifespans, and allowing the occasional seedling will make sure they persist in your garden.

Of the small, tight, mounding species, one of my favorites is *Dianthus glacialus*. True, the habit isn't as tight as some, but the floral display on this one is hard to beat. Clear, cotton candy–pink flowers are produced in such large quantities that they can almost completely cover the plant in spring. This is one plant that I do like to deadhead after bloom because the abundance of brown seedpods really detracts from enjoying the beautiful foliage the rest of the season.

When I'm looking for an architectural tight, tight mound, I like the selection 'Mini Mounds', both because the form is impeccable (though flowering is sparse) and because in my experience, it is one of the most robust of the tight mounding forms, less likely to rot out or otherwise fail to perform.

Also worth considering is *Dianthus deltoides*, which is the most mainstream of the really short dianthus. *Dianthus deltoides* is very lovely, forming a soft creeping mat of lush bright-green leaves, producing quite a different look from the hard, blue, dense mounds of the other small species. As the lusher, greener foliage would suggest, this species likes more water than the dense mounds and is much more tolerant of less-than-perfect drainage. It also spreads much faster and will seed around with abandon if you let it. Individual flowers are very small, produced in massive quantities in the spring, and in the best forms, a very rich, beautiful, saturated red. There are some named forms and several excellent seed strains—probably too aggressive and not dry-loving enough for the most elite part of your rock garden, but an excellent transition plant where the rock garden meets the heavier soil of other parts of the garden. It is also very pretty, very easy, and there is nothing wrong with either of those things.

Dianthus deltoides 'Flashing Lights' packs plenty of visual punch; just bear in mind that it seeds freely and needs regular moisture.

Drabas

above › *Draba aizoides* growing in habitat in the Tatra Mountains.

below › *Draba polytricha* in bloom forms a solid sheet of yellow.

For gardeners like myself who garden in the frigid North where winters are long and snowy, drabas in the rock garden are an absolute must, as they are consistently the first thing to come into bloom. The snow melts, the garden returns, and I, having gone absolutely insane with anticipation, haunt the garden daily. Most plants (wisely) sit still and wait for consistently warm weather to start growing and blooming. But in those early days of not-even-really-spring-yet, when nothing but snowdrops have shown themselves elsewhere in the garden, my sanity is saved when the drabas burst into bloom with solid sheets of yellow that completely cover the plants. If the weather stays cool the display can last for weeks, though it will be significantly shorter if warmer weather prevails. Though the sheets of screaming yellow between the rocks might be a bit vulgar at other times of year, in early spring, vulgar and bright is exactly what the doctor ordered.

Though bright in the mad rush of early spring bloom, once flowering is over drabas settle down into a much more refined look, forming classic rock garden buns—dense mounds of green undulating between rocks in the garden. This is a plant I recommend deadheading after flowering, as the seedpods are rather large and obtrusive. They're also held well above the foliage; trimming them back is quick and easy, leaving a pristine plant to enjoy the rest of the season.

Solid and undemanding performers, drabas are long-lived and quick to establish, putting down deep roots to give them impressive drought tolerance. They are generally tolerant of just about any abuse short of keeping them soggy at the crown all the time.

One word of advice, however, is that drabas rarely seem to look good at the nursery. In my time working at an alpine plants nursery, drabas were always easy to grow: they root from cuttings no problem, transplant and grow in nursery pots happily, and are tolerant of both under- and over-watering. But in the lusher conditions of fertilizer and water you use at a nursery to get a plant to size in something like a reasonable amount of time so as to (hopefully) avoid going out of business, drabas loose their tight, tidy form and get loose, rangy, and really rather unattractive looking. Don't let that put you off purchasing one—as soon as they settle into the lean soil and bright sun of the rock garden they quickly become dense and full, and will be an essential part of your annual celebration of the end of winter.

Though there are several commonly available species of *Draba* to choose from, they are largely similar in most aspects—the same yellow or white flowers and attractive green mounds of foliage. And from a gardener's standpoint, their most relevant differences are in their growth habit, with species like *Draba aizoides* forming tight, dense mounds with flowers produced close to the leaves, while *D. hispanica* is somewhat looser with longer leaves and flowers held more up above the foliage.

Erodiums

This genus often gets overshadowed by its better-known close relatives, geraniums and pelargoniums, but I personally think it has nicer plants than either of those genera. You can easily see the family resemblance in the flowers—simple, five-petaled, often marked with beautiful patterns. The rock garden erodiums form little shrub-lets with tiny gnarled stems a bit like those of pelargoniums, but shrunk down to the extreme. These are topped with often beautifully cut, fern-like leaves that range from green to silver, leaves good enough to make a killer garden feature even out of flower. But the really great aspect of these plants is that they are basically never out of flower. They start blooming in late spring and keep on keeping on right up until—and sometimes past—the first frost. Flowers aren't incredibly profuse; these aren't plants that cover themselves in a solid sheet of color, but that constant presence of bloom, especially in the summer and fall, is invaluable to keeping interest in the rock garden after the peak spring bloom.

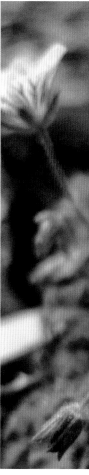

There is a dearth of information about winter hardiness of *Erodium*. I've grown many species which were listed as being hardy to zone 6 or 7, but have been perfectly hardy in my zone 5 garden, even sailing through two back-to-back winters from hell with lows of -26°F. The only species that I've found to be tender is *Erodium chamaedryoides*, which is a shame because it is an absolutely adorable, tiny little plant, mere inches tall, and constantly pumping out sweet pink flowers. It takes mild winters for me and should be hardy to zone 6. Of the species that are robustly and reliably hardy for me, one of my favorites is *E. chrysantha*, with pale-yellow flowers all summer long produced over a mass of silver leaves. It is one of the larger species, forming mounds up to 6 inches tall and eventually spreading out to a foot or more wide. *Erodium glandulosum* is another one of the best species, forming a low mound less than 6 inches tall made up of finely cut, ferny green leaves, and continuously topped with white or pale-pink flowers generously marked with big, dramatic purple splashes on the upper petals.

When it comes to culture, all these species have proved to be adaptable and easy to please. They appreciate good drainage but are not picky about it; short of an outright soggy situation they're fine. So any rock garden, even a less-than-perfectly built one, should work. Full sun is required for maximum flower production, but they'll live just fine in part shade if you simply

left › **The white and purple flowers of** *Erodium glandulosum* **are produced nearly continuously.**

above › *Erodium chamaedryoides* **is nearly perfect, though more tender than the other species.**

above right ›
Even without flowers, the fern-like foliage of *Erodium glandulosum* is well worth having in the garden.

below right ›
***Erodium chrysantha* produces its nearly white flowers continuously from spring to fall.**

want to enjoy them for the foliage. Add to that easygoing nature the fact that they root easily from cuttings, and erodiums can be perfect stand-by plants. Something to propagate a few extra pots of so you can plug them in when one of the drama queens of the rock garden has given up the ghost and you have a hole to fill.

I will leave you with one note of warning, however. Though all the species I've mentioned here are perfectly well behaved, never running or seeding around, there are some erodiums which are outright weeds: notably *E. cicutarium*, *E. botrys*, and to a slightly lesser extent, *E. carvifolium*. These plants are beautiful, with abundant magenta flowers and attractive cut foliage, but reproduce with great abandon to become weedy menaces. Steer clear of these and your erodium experience will be a wonderful one.

Gentians

To the gardener, gentian is synonymous with blue, and catalogs frequently describe other flowers as being gentian blue in an effort to lure you into buying them. These comparisons are rarely accurate, as true, rich blue is one of the rarest of colors for flowers, and almost nothing does it as well as *Gentiana*.

Gentiana is a big genus with quite a lot of variation, but the iconic member of the group, the plant most people have in mind when they say "gentian" with a note of longing in their voice, is *Gentiana acaulis* and a handful of closely related species. The tiny, tight mounds of glossy dark-green foliage are only inches tall, slowly forming a mat. Blooming in the spring—and often re-blooming in the summer or fall—they have absolutely massive flowers often nearly as big as the entire rest of the plant, an inch, sometimes two inches long; and a stunning, rich, saturated, true, true, blue, without even a hint of mauve or lavender or purple. As beautiful as they are, *G. acaulis* and related species gain an extra layer of allure thanks

Gentiana septemfida brings fresh color to the late-summer garden.

to being rather fussy. Well, in most climates. As a classic alpine plant they require good drainage, resent drying out, and particularly dislike hot, humid summer nights. They are just growable for me in Michigan, and though they don't tend to be long-lived nor heavy flowering, I was always rather proud of them—until I took a trip to Portland, Oregon, and visited Edelweiss Nursery, a wonderful alpine nursery near there, and saw flat upon flat of lush, happy plants growing away without a care in the world, producing more flowers in a fall re-bloom than my plants do in the spring. So if you are blessed with cool summers, by all means indulge in these wonderful plants. For those of us with a more continental climate they're usually not the best choice. If you do want to try the acaulis gentians, the most adaptable species in the group is *Gentiana angustifolia*, which is a little taller than *G. acaulis*, and when happy will make large mats covered with dazzling blue flowers. So give it a go, and if you succeed move on to *G. acaulis* itself in all its beautiful forms.

Much easier to grow in less ideal conditions are the selections and hybrids of *Gentiana paradoxa* and *G. septemfida*. These two species are very much confused in the trade, and much of what is sold as either of them is actually hybrids of the two. But I don't mind much the purity of the species as these are stellar plants, hybrid or not. Despite not boasting the elite, difficult status of the acaulis types, I think these are more attractive plants. Flowers are smaller, maybe half the size of an acaulis bloom, and the plants larger—stems reaching 6 inches or so long, and trailing along the ground or over the edges of rock and containers if given a chance. I think the smaller flowers and larger plants look more in scale and a little less ridiculous then the acaulis types. At least that is what I tell myself in order to fight down my raging jealously for gardeners with milder summers than mine. The other thing I love about them is that they bloom—as the name *septemfida* suggests—in late summer and early fall, and I seriously adore late summer-fall bloomers. The overwhelming majority of rock garden plants bloom in spring and early summer, and the fall gentians are a very welcome addition, bringing their brilliant blue flowers to enliven the fall garden. They are especially welcome as the blue contrasts so marvelously with the yellow, orange, and red tones that tend to dominate in the fall.

Culture for *G. septemfida*, *G. paradoxa*, and their hybrids is fairly easy. They like good drainage, plenty of sun, and they don't want to dry out too much, but in all of those requirements are far from fussy. Winter-hardy in zone 3, they are significantly more heat tolerant than the acaulis gentians, but still don't love the Deep South. Thanks to their tendency to trail, they are perfect when planted at the edge of a container or bed where they can weep down dramatically.

Though there are named forms out there, many of the plants you'll see for sale are seedlings. Given that most of them are also hybrids, they're quite variable: colors ranging from light to dark blues, even the occasional white; different flower sizes, sometimes intricately fringed between the petals; and quite a range of flowering times, the earliest kicking off for me in August, while the latest wait until September or even October. When happy they seed around quite a bit—which is really hard to be upset about. As with all variable self-sowers, I recommend aggressively deadheading your least favorite forms and colors and letting the ones you like best seed around so that over time your garden will fill with the forms that match your personal taste.

left › *Gentiana acaulis* flowers are some of the most beautiful in the rock gardening world.

below › *Gentiana angustifolia* is the easiest of the Acaulis Group.

Hostas

As a young gardener, I lumped hostas in my mind with 'Stella d'Oro' daylilies and groundcover junipers. Boring, over-planted, and generally blah. Then on one of my first visits as a customer to Arrowhead Alpines, the nursery where I used to work, I saw of pot of 'Pandora's Box', a hosta quite unlike any I had seen before. Beautiful leaves only a couple of inches tall painted with a bold white center and a crisp green edge, and to top it off, extremely showy dark purple flowers. I was smitten. Apparently I wasn't the only one: 'Pandora's Box' is the variegated sport of the (also delightful) *Hosta* 'Baby Bunting', and its arrival on the market in 1996 sparked the beginning of intense interest in small hostas and a flurry of marvelous wee hostas have been produced since.

Little hostas are similar to their larger brethren; though as a rule of thumb, the smaller they are, the fussier they are. The larger of the smaller hostas, like the ever-popular (and ever-mutating) 'Blue Mouse Ears', are as easy and uncomplaining as the big standard hostas. The smallest ones, like

Hosta 'Blue Mouse Ears' looking stunning alongside *Gentiana septemfida* at the New York Botanical Garden.

that exquisite 'Pandora's Box', require a little more care. Primarily they want better drainage and thrive best in loose, sandy soils. In other words the tiny hostas want rock garden conditions, which is marvelous because that is exactly how they look best. Supremely well adapted to containers, they also thrive in raised beds and shady rock gardens of all sorts.

As with all hostas, the little ones will tolerate deep shade but really do best in bright, dappled shade. They have few pests beyond deer, slugs, and snails. One of the great advantages to growing little hostas in rock garden–type conditions is that the good drainage and especially sharp gravel mulches keep things drier and make for unhappy slugs and snails.

left › **Rock garden with hostas in Mike and Kathy Shadrack's western New York garden.**

right › **'Baby Bunting' is one of the smallest blue-leaved hostas.**

Deer, of course, are a perennial problem for the hosta lover, though tucking a tiny hosta into a crevice between rocks can keep their leaves out of reach of hungry mouths.

The hosta world moves quickly, with insane quantities of new varieties being released every year from both professional and amateur breeders. The sheer number of options to choose from can be overwhelming, so I turned to my dear friends Kathy and Mike Shadrack, coauthors of *The Book of Little Hostas*, to recommend some of their favorite varieties.

Start with 'Blue Mouse Ears', a terrific, vigorous hosta with small, glaucous-blue, very thick leaves. It seems very prone to chance mutations

Tiny, perfect, and notoriously fussy, 'Pandora's Box' is the first hosta to ever capture my heart.

resulting in a whole host of beautiful varieties with the same great, tough growth habit in different patterns. Of the many options within this sport family: Mike likes 'Mini Skirt', which has broad white leaf margins, while Kathy loves 'Dancing Mouse', all green with rippled leaves, and 'Snow Mouse', with white-centered leaves and much easier to grow than the similar looking but notoriously difficult 'Pandora's Box'.

If you want yellow leaves, 'Dragon Tails' was high on both Mike's and Kathy's lists, and is one of my favorites as well—long, narrow chartreuse leaves with a beautiful rippled margin. A similar look with a narrow green edge to the leaves is the lovely 'Green Eyes', and 'Lakeside Down Sized' has chartreuse leaves with a narrow white margin.

For really tiny plants only a few inches tall, 'Baby Bunting' has beautiful glaucous-blue leaves, and its sports 'Cherish' and 'Pandora's Box', with cream- and white-centered leaves respectively. Notoriously fussy, they're spectacular when happy.

Irises

Iris is a massive genus, home to some of the most beautiful and important garden plants, and the list of possible species and groups to use in the rock garden is long. But for my money, there are two groups of irises that are easy to grow, beautiful, and absolutely essential for the rock garden: the dwarf bearded irises and the Reticulata Group of bulbous irises.

DWARF BEARDED IRISES

Bearded irises need no introduction, and for good reason. They're spectacularly tough, beautiful, and easy to grow. The typical tall bearded varieties are rather too large for the rock garden, and the newer hybrids have been bred to such a frenzy of frothy, frilly petals as to be quite revolting and not suitable for much of anything except iris shows. The dwarf beardeds, however, are quite another matter. The American Iris Society classifies standard dwarf beardeds as being between 8 and 16 inches tall, while miniature dwarf beardeds are 8 inches or less—both sizes perfectly suited to the

rock garden. There are a number of beautiful species in this group that are well worth growing. *Iris suaveolens* in particular has many forms, all quite lovely, forming tiny mats of leaves with oversized flowers fully half again as tall as the entire rest of the plant, and the newer hybrids are quite lovely as well. Breeding work widened the color range significantly, and produced varieties with graceful, elegant, well-balanced flowers. No doubt in a decade or two they'll be just as fouled up as the tall beardeds, but for now you can get lovely new hybrids that give you significantly more vigor and better performance than the species, and still look natural and completely at home in a rock garden full of other wild species.

 Culture of the bearded irises is so easy as to be ridiculous. Full sun gives the best flowering, plant the rhizomes right at the soil surface, and give them decent drainage. That's about it. During the summer they go semi-dormant and can take extremely hot, dry, conditions without blinking. The one serious insect pest is the iris borer, which can be a problem.

left › **Masses of dwarf bearded iris at Royal Botanic Garden Edinburgh.**

right › *Iris* **'Giggles and Grins'.**

The females lay eggs in the fall, which overwinter on old leaves and stems; so thoroughly cleaning up all old foliage in the fall after a few hard frosts (when egg laying is finished) and destroying it will effectively limit your population of borers.

There are so many excellent varieties to choose from, but a few of my favorites are 'Red at Last', which really is almost the elusive true-red

bearded iris; 'Giggles and Grins', and 'Clown Pants', both of which I love almost as much for the happy names as for the cheerful and unique color patterns of the flowers.

RETICULATA GROUP OF BULBOUS IRISES

This is one of my cannot-live-without-it groups of plants. Bulbous irises like *Iris reticulata* are spectacularly beautiful, to my eyes perhaps the loveliest of all the irises. The flowers are notably graceful and long-limbed, vividly colored in shades of blue, purple, and yellow (with a whole host of new colors on the way), and sweetly fragrant if you get down to smelling range, or enjoy them in a vase (where they do beautifully, by the by). All of that, and they bloom so early in the spring most years that I can make a mixed bouquet of them with snowdrops, which is saying something. Snowdrops are frankly pretty dull flowers. I adore them because they are so early, resolutely blooming when the rest of the garden is pretty boring, but the dwarf bulbous irises bloom very nearly as early, and are flat-out spectacular. I love them for their early, early display when I'm itching for anything happening in the garden, but the other terrific thing about their growth habit is that they very quickly go dormant and totally vanish. The foliage is narrow and grass-like, not particularly noticeable after flowering is over, and it browns up and is gone completely before you know it, meaning the bulbous irises are perfect for planting—preferably by the hundreds—in an already full garden. By the time other perennials are up or cushions are flowering, it will be as if they were never there.

Miniature dwarf bearded iris 'Red at Last'.

Culture is easy—even in my cool, wet, climate many of them will grow well and increase even in normal garden conditions. When treated to the drier, warmer home of a rock garden, they go nuts, bulking quickly into a spectacular carpet of early spring color.

For a long time, the forms of these irises you could get were *Iris reticulata*, *I. danfordiae*, and a handful of hybrids like the dark-wine 'George' or the pale blue with dramatic yellow markings of 'Cantab'. These hybrids are lovely, and also sadly totally sterile—the end of the line. But there is a revolution afoot in the world of these irises, created single-handedly by Alan McMurtrie, a passionate backyard breeder in Toronto, Canada. Working with little-known species, he's created a new line of fertile hybrids, and the colors and forms he's getting out of these hybrid populations are absolutely out of this world. Coppers and browns and golds and stunning blues, intricately patterned, these spectacular plants are still difficult to locate commercially, but hopefully soon they'll be as widespread as they deserve.

Lewisias

The genus is named for Lewis, as in Lewis and Clark, the pioneering explorers of the American West. Clark got *Clarkia* named after him, and both are extremely lovely genera, but I rather think Lewis got the better genus. Lewisias are some of the most strikingly beautiful plants for the rock garden. Some rock garden plants are the sort of thing that appeal only to the experts and obsessive collectors, beautiful for their detailed tiny forms and structures. Lewisias, however, are not that sort of plant at all. When in full bloom in the spring, they are show stoppers with masses of huge, brilliantly colored flowers ranging from screaming magentas and scarlets to delicate pinks, pale yellows, wonderful salmons, and warm, soft oranges. Visiting gardens in Denver with masses of them self-sowing around (they do that in Colorado), I heard from gardeners that when lewisias are in full bloom, the whole neighborhood is talking about them.

Lewisia is an exclusively western America genus, native to a wide range of scattered habitats

above › *Lewisia cotyledon.*

below › **The easy and adaptable** *Lewisia* 'Pinkie'.

in those hot, dry mountains. Though often found in cooler, moister micro-climates in the mountains, they're still highly adapted to harsh condi-tions. They have thick, fleshy, succulent leaves—the better to resist drying out—and many species go into a dormant stage during the heat of the sum-mer to conserve water. Some species, like the lovely *L. rediviva*, drop their leaves entirely and retreat to a thick, fleshy, carrot-like root which, though

apparently unpleasant enough to earn it the common name of "bitterroot," was harvested as a food source by Native Americans. Other species, like the most common one in gardens, *L. cotyledon*, stay evergreen year-round, though still go into a semi-dormant resting phase in hot, dry weather.

If you are lucky enough to live in a climate similar to where lewisias are native, they're an easy garden plant. They'll rejoice in a little supplemental water during the growing season, and seed around impressively and easily. Individual plants, even in the most ideal garden circumstances, are often a bit short-lived; you would be wise to occasionally re-propagate them by taking the side rosettes as cuttings, which will allow you to preserve exceptional individuals. Or plant out seedlings, which is always fun because it allows you to select for flower forms and colors you like, and while you are at it, select those that thrive better in your climate.

In wetter climates, like where I garden, lewisias need special care. Highly adapted to dry conditions, they are very prone to rotting in rainy climates. The biggest problem seems to be water coming from above. They are found in the wild most often in areas where the wind collects deep snow packs that melt slowly over the course of the summer, providing water at the soil level but not on the leaves. Those tightly packed rosettes of succulent leaves tend to hold water pretty well when it rains, which in turn leads to rot. Best results are with very sharp-draining soil, and many good growers swear by planting them in a rock wall or other position where the rosette can sit on its side, preventing water from puddling in the leaves. They also do very well in an alpine house and are rather brilliant in containers that can be moved into a garage or under an eave in the winter to keep off excess water.

Despite the succulent, water-saving leaves that usually signal a plant that demands full sun, lewisias tend to favor north slopes in the wild; in particularly hot, humid climates they will welcome some light afternoon shade.

There are many species of *Lewisia*, but relatively few are widely grown. *Lewisia cotyledon* is *the* lewisia, the most common, and the source of virtually all available selections. It has quite beautiful succulent foliage, and large, brightly colored flowers; but perhaps most important, it is extremely variable in the wild, with several distinct varieties. All these varieties

Masses of self-sowing *Lewisia cotyledon* in the garden of Lee Curtis in Denver, Colorado, where lewisias are so happy they're nearly weeds.

interbreed with abandon in cultivation, and that initial wild variability has been amplified many times over by plant breeders around the world. Modern seed strains have enormous flowers: colors range from pale pink to the darkest magenta to bright yellow, with some excellent melon, salmon, and orange forms in between, with each petal often shading between multiple colors. Leaf shape is just as variable, and though that has received less attention from breeders, you'll still find forms with dramatically waved or even ruffled leaf margins that are extremely attractive. A lot of the breeding work has taken place in the United Kingdom, Ashwood Nurseries being one of the leading lights of that work. The many generations these plants have spent in the unique cool and wet British climate has caused them to adapt to thrive in those same conditions. In fact, *L. cotyledon* has proved just as mutable in its ability to thrive in different climates as it has in its wide-ranging flower forms. Betty Ann Davidson in Minneapolis and the late Carl Gehennio of Pittsburgh in the United States (both continental climates with hot, humid summers and cold, wet winters that are not traditionally good growing conditions for lewisias), have developed strains and cultivars of *L. cotyledon* that thrive in that climate. Sadly, neither selections seem to be commercially available any longer, but there is a great opportunity for gardeners everywhere to start with diverse hybrid strains, such as those from Ashwood, and select the survivors over generations to develop forms that will thrive in your local conditions, whatever they may be.

Though *Lewisia cotyledon* dominates the lewisia world, other species are worth growing as well. *Lewisia longipetala* is far less showy than *L. cotyledon*, with significantly smaller flowers in pale pink. It is a lovely little thing, perhaps more tasteful and natural looking than the highly bred *L. cotyledon* varieties, and is also more adaptable to conditions in the eastern United States than *L. cotyledon*. This species is best known perhaps in its hybrids with *L. cotyledon*. Look out for older hybrids like 'Pinkie', and the newer hybrid seed strains 'Little Plum', 'Little Peach', and 'Little Mango'. They don't have quite the massive flowers and bright colors of pure cotyledon, but they grow vigorously and easily for me.

Penstemons

Penstemon is a primarily New World genus, with the highest concentration of its some 245 species native to the western United States. On the slopes of the Rocky Mountains and the many dry habitats of the steppe regions around them, a great number of lovely penstemons have evolved—small, compact forms perfectly suitable for the rock garden. While some rock plants are all about the foliage and form of the sculptural mounds, penstemons are all about the flowers—and what flowers they have! Colors range from brilliant true blues to bright red and scarlet, to yellow, pink, white, and everything in between. Most flower heavily somewhere around late spring to early summer; quite a few will re-bloom on through the rest of the summer, making them an invaluable way to extend the season of bloom past the typically spring-heavy bloom in most rock gardens.

Penstemons, nearly universally, have one strict requirement for their culture: they don't like to be soggy. Before I really understood that, I killed an embarrassing number of them in the heavy, wet

left › The most common form of *Penstemon pinifolius* is a cheerful scarlet.

right › *Penstemon davidsonii* var. *menziesii* has a flower production few plants can match.

clay of my previous garden. Move them into the good drainage of a rock garden, however, and most are easy and adaptable. Thanks to impressively deep root systems, they're quite drought tolerant. Unlike many true alpines, the small species native to dry areas at lower elevations thrive in summer heat, though some will resent the hot humid nights of the southeastern United States.

Getting penstemons with the correct name can be difficult. For one, the genus is a taxonomic battleground between splitters (taxonomists who want to designate every little local variant as a different species) and lumpers (who want to combine the multitude of species named by the splitters into fewer, more diverse species). Aside from that, penstemons are a bit like columbines for sheer promiscuity. If you have multiple penstemons in your garden, there is a good chance that a lot of the seed produced will be hybrid. That isn't always a bad thing—it can be lots of fun to see what you get, but do plan on taking the species names of seeds donated by gardeners to seed exchanges with a grain of possibly hybridized salt.

With a huge number of options to choose from, you can explore penstemons for the rest of your gardening life, and there are a lot of great ones to try. *Penstemon caespitosus* 'Claude Barr' is named for a pioneering rock gardener in South Dakota who realized that though his hot, extreme

'Mercer Yellow'
is a nice yellow
selection of
*Penstemon
pinifolius.*

weather was inimical to most true alpines, many native plants had similar small, compact forms that were perfectly suited to the rock gardening style. 'Claude Barr', the plant, is a perfect example of this—a tiny, trailing, groundcovering species growing flat to the ground, usually less than an inch tall but spreading widely, and blooming heavily with lavender-blue flowers. Because this plant will root down as it spreads, it can get quite wide; it is perhaps too aggressive for the smallest of rock gardens but looks stunning creeping between large boulders or trailing over the edge of a raised bed or large trough.

Similar, or perhaps even nicer, is *P. davidsonii* var. *menziesii*, which can bloom to the point of all but completely obscuring the foliage. It isn't as inclined to re-bloom later in the summer, and it's a little fussier in demanding perfect drainage through the winter months.

One of my other favorite penstemons is *P. pinifolius*, which is very different in looks than most of the other species suitable for the rock garden. The species name *pinifolius* means "pine leaf," and it is well named, as the evergreen leaves do indeed look like little narrow needles. The plant is on the large side, around a foot tall, but forms a lovely dense mound. Best of all, it blooms nearly nonstop all summer with long, trumpet-shaped flowers in—depending on the selection—shades of red, orange, or yellow.

Polygalas

Polygala is an unusual genus with quite a diversity of species, including two species with which I am deeply in love and think should be in every rock garden.

Polygala chamaebuxus is appealing year-round, forming a very low—only 6 to 8 inches tall—creeping shrub with glossy evergreen foliage that looks wonderful growing its way between rocks. The foliage always looks good but the real show comes in late winter (in mild climates) to early spring, with masses of charmingly odd flowers, which I've seen described as resembling snapdragons, pea flowers, or orchids, but really look like nothing but themselves. The blooms are either white or, in the common selection 'Kamniski', bright magenta, with two big flaring wing-like petals and a little sticking-out nose of contrasting bright yellow that turns a warm orange as the flower ages. Better yet, expect occasional repeat bloom in the summer if happy, and those brilliantly colored, uniquely formed flowers are fragrant as well.

Fully hardy to USDA zone 5, *Polygala chamaebuxus* is tough and easy to grow provided it has the good drainage a typical rock garden gives it. Blooming will be heaviest with full sun, but it will tolerate partial shade as well. Though often reported as preferring acidic soil, it is perfectly happy in my slightly alkaline soil. In short, this is one of those adaptable plants that will be happy in almost every garden. Which makes it all the more strange how infrequently it is grown.

above › *Polygala chamaebuxus* in riotous bloom.

right › **The true blue of *Polygala calcarea*.**

The only thing perhaps even better than *Polygala chamaebuxus* is *P. calcarea*. Smaller in all respects, *P. calcarea* is just an inch or two tall, and only slowly spreading, but with the same beautiful evergreen foliage. As the species name suggests, it grows in the wild among limestone rocks, and so is very happy in alkaline conditions in the garden but certainly it doesn't demand them, and generally is as easy and carefree as you could wish. Flowering is in midspring, and also when it shows its superiority (to my taste anyway) to *P. chamaebuxus*. The individual flowers are smaller but produced in prodigious quantity, completely covering the plant in a solid sheet of tiny flowers. Best of all is their color, that most elusive flower color of all: true, clear, perfect blue without even a hint of purple or lavender.

Both these species are easily propagated from seed or cuttings, so if you can't find any for sale, make friends with someone who has them in their garden and beg piteously until you get a piece to grow for yourself. Believe me when I say that any amount of groveling is worth it for these plants.

Primulas

The genus *Primula* is huge and diverse, but the real rock garden primroses consist of *P. auricula*, *P. allionii*, *P. marginata*, and a few related species.

These primroses are clearly different from the more commonly seen species and hybrids typically grown in cool, moist, shaded conditions. Alpine primroses like more sun and good drainage, and you can see the difference in their leaves. Unlike the thin, delicately textured leaves of most primroses, the alpine primulas have thick, fleshy, almost succulent leaves, often covered with a layer of powdery white called farina. The thick leaves obviously help store water, and the farina reflects off excess sunlight to protect the leaves from burning and drying out. One of the cool things about farina is that it will wash off. Run a watering can over a primrose with very silvery leaves, and you'll see it rinsing away onto the soil. It doesn't all wash away at once, but regular overhead watering or rainfall will reduce the amount of silver on the leaves considerably. This is a very effective adaptation: in dry weather the leaves stay silvery

Auriculas exhibit a range of colors that is nothing short of dazzling.

A yellow border auricula.

to prevent the sun from burning off too much precious moisture, but when it rains, the farina sunblock washes away so that the leaves can photosynthesize most effectively with the abundant water. Most plants adjust their leaves in response to sunlight and water, growing smaller, thicker ones in hot dry conditions and bigger, thinner leaves in wet, shady sites. But growing new leaves takes time, while farina washing off in a rainstorm allows for instant adaptation to grow best in the current conditions.

Though the primrose is perfectly happy to shed unneeded farina upon the arrival of rain, the gardener is not always so thrilled. The silvery leaves of many of these varieties are extremely beautiful, and more significantly, many varieties of alpine primroses also have white farina on their flowers. In this case, the point in terms of plant survival is not as clear, but the practical reality is the same: many of the alpine primroses, especially the auricula varieties bred for the show bench, have thick farina forming a very striking white eye to the flower—a white eye that is quickly washed away by a strong rainstorm or a gardener with a hose. For this reason, obsessive primrose growers like to keep their plants under cover—especially when they are in flower—to maintain the brightest white eye.

This group of primroses has proved to be one of the toughest and easiest to grow in my garden. Most primroses deeply resent hot, dry weather, but the thick, fleshy leaves make these primroses very well suited to drier conditions. In my garden in Michigan, they thrive in anything from nearly full sun to light shade, and are tolerant of a wide range of soils. Waterlogged soil isn't good, and they do grow well in slightly richer, moister soils than the true alpine plants. But for me they thrive in a wide range of conditions, even performing quite beautifully in the parched dry shade under a silver maple tree with no supplemental watering. In very sunny climates, such as Colorado, they prefer light shade. The auricula types in particular have a very long history of breeding and growing in the United Kingdom, but they honestly do seem to grow and perform better in climates with warmer, drier summers. All these primroses do beautifully in containers as well, either mixed with other plants in a trough or showcased alone in a pot by themselves.

'Joan Hughes' demonstrating the allionii habit of producing a solid dome of flowers.

Primula auricula is a lovely little species, but the auricula primroses of horticulture are *Primula ×pubescens*, a hybrid between *P. auricula* and *P. hirsuta*. This hybrid produces plants with wide, rounded, fleshy evergreen leaves that reach maybe 6 to 8 inches tall, and heads of lightly fragrant flowers that can be very nearly any color you can imagine. This hybrid has a long record and is a popular show plant with all the sort of strange history that plants bred extensively for flower shows develop. Specific rules for what a show auricula is "supposed to" look like means breeding was focused deeply on rich, bright colors, perfectly rounded petals, and bright white centers of farina (often called for some reason, "paste" centers), along with breeding for rather cool—or possibly just odd, depending on your point of view—forms with green, grey, and black flowers. Again, as is typical with plants bred for flower shows, these varieties tend not to be very good growers, demanding coddling with carefully constructed potting composts and alpine houses to shelter them from the rain that threatens to wash away the white farina centers of their flowers.

Far easier to grow, though not as perfect in form, are the "border auriculas," which have been selected for performance in the garden rather than the show bench. Highly variable, these usually don't have the precisely rounded petals of the show primroses, nor the thick farina, but are generally tougher, more vigorous plants, better suited to general garden use. All of them are absolutely lovely; most notably I feel for a certain unique quality to the flower colors. Rarely is an auricula primrose a simple pink or red or blue.

They're delightful muted mauves and tans and rosy salmons—rich, sophisticated colors worthy of a celebrity line of paint colors or a high-fashion gown. Add to that a delightful fragrance, beautiful fleshy, evergreen foliage, and a habit of re-blooming in late summer, and you've got a spectacular group of plants. Given the scarcity of the elite named forms, the best way to acquire truly spectacular auriculas is to buy a big packet of seed, grow them out, and select the ones that thrill you the most; or if you are lucky enough to find one near you, go to a nursery that grows a lot of the seed strains in the spring when they are in flower and pick out the forms you like best from those.

Primula marginata.

If *Primula auricula* is too large for you, consider *Primula allionii* and related species. Like the auriculas, many of the plants sold as *Primula allionii* selections are hybrids of various small species, or even crosses with the auriculas. These plants are the truly tiny alpine primrose, the smallest ones forming rosettes of leaves ranging from an inch or two tall down to—in the very smallest forms—half an inch or even smaller. Like the auriculas, leaves are thick and fleshy, though they usually lack farina and are sometimes covered with a light dusting of fuzz. The flowers have a more limited color

A border auricula happy in a dry, lightly shaded spot in my garden.

range than the auriculas, probably merely because they weren't as popular with the breeders and flower shows as the auriculas; most of them range from white to pink to magenta and purples, though there are a few with yellow tones to them. When they are in bloom, very few things can match them for sheer flower profusion. The flowers are very large for the size of the plant and held right above the foliage; they can totally cover the plant, producing a solid dome of blooms very early in the spring, with some forms showing a tendency to re-bloom lightly in the late summer.

Culturally, allionii primroses are a little more demanding than their larger auricula cousins. They generally appreciate light shade and well-drained soil that never totally dries out, and they can be a little fussier about winter cold and wet. Their tiny size makes them absolutely perfect specimens for a container or trough.

And finally, I can't leave alpine primroses without mentioning perhaps my favorite, *Primula marginata*, which boasts the most beautiful silvery leaves with a dramatic saw-tooth edge, a trait particularly pronounced in selections like 'Napoleon'. Flowers are an elegant, clear lavender-blue, and in all other respects it looks and grows like an auricula, plants that it indeed hybridizes with easily. It is awesome.

Pulsatillas

Pulsatilla is a wide-ranging genus, with species native to Europe, North America, and Asia. With such a wide range, it has unsurprisingly acquired a number of common names: pasque flower, prairie crocus, and meadow anemone. Wild forms are usually in shades of blue and purple, with several selected varieties—mostly from the European species, *Pulsatilla vulgaris*—in other colors including white, pinks, and reds and in forms with fringed petal edges and semi-double flowers.

Though not strictly an alpine genus, pulsatillas love good drainage and full sun in the garden and so thrive in rock garden conditions. They're also invaluable in the garden because they are one of the first, showiest flowers of spring (hence the name prairie crocus). As beautiful as those early flowers are, I think I may like them even better when the bloom finishes and each nodding flower turns upward and the developing seed heads grow into marvelous silky brushes that give a wonderful vertical accent and contrast to the dominating low forms of most rock gardens. In my garden some

A nice dark form of *Pulsatilla vulgaris*.

left › **Pulsatilla going to seed may be even prettier than in flower.**

above › *Pulsatilla turczaninovii.*

varieties will throw an odd late summer re-bloom after the main spring bloom, nothing as spectacular as the spring, but still a welcome addition to the summer garden.

Pulsatilla vulgaris has a reputation for sulking in hot summer continental climates in North America. Gardeners there would be better served by the North American native *P. patens*, which ranges in the wild from Texas up into Canada, particularly if you can find a native form near to where you garden. As with many such wide-ranging species, there are often huge differences between forms from the northern and southern ends of the range.

above right ›
*Pulsatilla
regeliana.*

below › **A red
*Pulsatilla
vulgaris* hybrid.**

I'll confess that most pulsatilla species look pretty much the same to me, but there is one I am very fond of that is distinctly different and unique, with the tongue-twisting name of *Pulsatilla turczaninovii*. Usually I'm a big advocate for Latin names all the time, but with a mouthful of a name like that you'd be forgiven for calling it the Siberian pasque flower. The blooms are smaller than those of many pulsatillas, but a lovely shade of dark blue; the form is unusual, narrow in a way that reminds me of a tulip, with the tips of the petals rolling back.

Ramondas

I have to admit that a lot of the appeal to me of ramondas is the fact that they are related to, and look a great deal like, African violets. But unlike their houseplant relatives, which shrivel up and die at the mere thought of chilly weather, ramondas are fully winter-hardy into zone 5. There is something so satisfying about growing a plant that looks like it would never survive.

Tony Reznicek, a rock gardening wizard who lives near me in Michigan and grows beautiful ramondas, describes their culture as easy but specific. In other words, if you put them in the right spot they'll never give you a moment's trouble, settling in and producing their beautiful rosettes of crinkled dark green leaves and big displays of lavender, African violet–like flowers in late spring. Put them in the wrong spot, however, and they'll be dead faster than you can imagine. In nature they grow in shaded north-facing limestone crevices where they never get direct sun, but plenty of bright, indirect light. In the garden you can give them these conditions by simply tucking them

The purple African violet–like blooms of *Ramonda myconi* in the foreground of a flowery rock garden.

into a crevice on the north side of a bed or wall or crevice garden, where the direct sun never shines. In wet, rainy climates you'd be best to make sure they're growing on a steep angle as well, so that water can't collect in the base of the leaf rosette and cause them to rot. Satisfy those conditions, and they'll thrive. Move them to where they get hit by a direct blast of the sun, and they'll be dead in no time.

This hatred of direct sun makes ramondas an invaluable addition to the shaded rock garden, both for their great foliage and their abundant flowers, which can be all too often lacking in the shade.

Ramondas are sometimes called resurrection plants for their ability to recover rapidly and seemingly miraculously from extreme desiccation. In their native habitats water is available from fall through spring but it is extremely dry in the summer; in response, they simply dry down completely and wait for the rains to return. Luckily, they don't demand this extreme dry period, and if kept watered through the summer will continue to grow and look beautiful. If you live somewhere with a seasonal dry period, you can simply let them shrivel up to return to growth with the arrival of water.

Another great thing about ramondas is that they, like their African violet cousins, will root from leaf cuttings; so once you've got a great plant, sharing it with your gardening friends is as easy as can be. Seed is also sometimes available, but be warned that the seeds are as fine as dust and need to be grown very carefully to prevent them from ever drying out once they germinate. They spend an inordinate amount of time as a tiny, tiny, fussy seedling before putting on enough size to cope with the world. Far easier to stick with leaf cuttings when you can.

While there are three different species of *Ramonda*, all three are largely similar from a horticultural point of view, with the same crinkled leaves and pale lavender to white flowers, and only *R. myconi* is regularly available for sale. There is a "pink" selection of *R. myconi*, though it is more of a pinkish-lavender than a true, strong pink.

above › *Ramonda* in Tony Reznicek's Michigan garden adds a beautiful foliage accent even before coming into full spring bloom.

below › A mass of *Ramonda myconi* in full bloom.

Saxifrages

Saxifraga, which when at home, generally goes by "sax" (though be warned, there are some people in this world with misguided priorities who, when they hear "sax," think saxophone rather than saxifrage), is a massive genus of a few hundred species, highly variable, and very many of them extremely desirable garden plants. It is an incredibly diverse group of plants, and various species provide some of the most exceptional foliage and floral displays in the rock garden.

261

An unnamed mossy sax selection.

Let's break it down into the main groups: silver saxes, dwarf cushion saxes, and mossy saxes. But first, there is also a little-grown—at least in the West—group of fall-blooming saxifrages from Asia that boast incredibly beautiful dark foliage and huge masses of pink or white flowers. I've never grown them, but seeing several selections in Glenn Shapiro's garden, I've fallen deeply in love, particularly with *Saxifraga fortunei* 'Black Ruby', with almost black leaves and brilliant-pink flowers.

SILVER SAXES

The silver saxes are so called because they are the most notable group of the genus that has odd little glands called hydathodes that produce the most marvelous brilliant-white crystals of lime on the leaves. Presumably the function is to protect the foliage from the heat of intense sunlight, but the effect in the garden is quite striking and unusual, looking like nothing more than a particularly beautiful coating of hoarfrost. Frost can be a lovely thing in the garden, and we've all seen—and perhaps taken—stunning photos of a leaf or flower or twig outlined with frost crystals on a sunny morning. Few things are more beautiful, but those photos capture an unpredictable, fleeting, and rather uncomfortable cold moment. The silver saxes look that way all the time, absolutely year-round, so you don't have to rush out and capture the moment first thing on a frosty morning; you can park it in a trough or bed and show it off to everyone who visits your garden. (Though, to be honest, frost-glazed silver saxes are a whole other level of awesome beauty.)

There are about (depending on whom you ask) a dozen species in this group along with a few hybrids, and they are almost without exception beautiful and very easy to grow. Less fussy for me than many of the hybrid mounded saxes I'll discuss later, they want good drainage but accept my rainy, cold climate without a second thought. In cooler climates they are happy in sun, but in hot summer gardens they are plants for a lightly shaded, somewhat wetter spot.

Particularly worth growing is *Saxifraga longifolia*. Massive rosettes of long, narrow leaves edged with silver, it is lovely in leaf; after maybe 5 or 6 years it sends up an absolutely over-the-top, huge spike of white flowers. The only downside is that it puts so much into that one over-the-top floral display that it expires immediately afterward. It is, however, very easy to grow from seed and will self-sow when happy.

DWARF CUSHION SAXES

This is perhaps the biggest section of the genus, with 100-plus species and hundreds more hybrids and cultivars. Some of the species produce the lime crusting on their leaves like the silver saxes, and the group also boasts species with very large flowers ranging from white to red to yellow, and

above › *Saxifraga longifolia.*

below › *Saxifraga sempervirens.*

all sorts—especially in the hybrid forms—of delightful oranges, creams, peaches, and everything else in between. There is no blue to be found, but short of that, the color range is pretty much covered. The main focus of breeding and growing these species has been in Europe, especially the United Kingdom. The results are stunning plants, most of which don't adapt particularly well to conditions in continental climates like most of the United States.

Though not as brightly colored as some of the others, *Saxifraga sempervirens* is one of the best in my opinion, being amenable to cultivation, flowering heavily with brilliant white to pale pink flowers on stems that are stained a deep purple.

left › *Saxifraga fortunei* 'Black Ruby'.

above › **An unnamed silver sax in Glenn Shapiro's garden.**

MOSSY SAXES

A very beautiful subgroup, one that was the absolute epitome of style and the newest and hottest thing in the early 1900s. The mossy saxes form tight mounds, mats, and domes of soft rich-green foliage that does, indeed, remind one of moss; if, that is, moss bloomed in early spring with large

and abundant flowers in shades of pink. The mossy saxes are indeed very lovely, and want cooler, wetter, and somewhat shadier conditions than the other saxes. They're a perfect choice for a lightly shaded rock garden, or if you want to create a rock garden–style garden but don't have the sun and drainage needed to grow some of the more typical rock garden plants.

Mossy saxes are also quite amenable to typical nursery conditions and so are widely available, often without a proper name attached. Which is a shame, because I've honestly yet to see a mossy sax I didn't like.

Sempervivums

above ›
Sempervivums.

below › **Cobweb
semps on a wall.**

I love these plants for a lot of reasons, not least
because of their name: *sempervivum* means "live
forever," which is a promising name for a plant! It
also abbreviates nicely to "semp," which is what
I usually call them, and they have a host of very
appealing common names: hen and chicks (cute),
roof leek (?), and welcome home husband be
he never so drunk (!). Though I have my doubts
about that last one; I've read it listed as a common
name many times, but I doubt that anyone has
ever called a plant that. A bit of a mouthful.

Whatever you call them, semps have one
charming attribute: they grow. They, as the name
suggests, don't die. They are also the perfect plant
to share, as the side rosettes (the chicks of the
name hen and chicks) can merely be pulled off and
handed to someone, thrown into a bag for the trip
home, tossed carelessly onto some soil, and they'll
grow on happily. Even better, they're not aggressive. They don't run around eating gardens and
weaker plants for breakfast; rather they generally
increase steadily, making a small dense mat, which

can, if you need it to, be transformed into hundreds of plants at moment's notice.

Most semps are so cheerfully adaptable that they get placed in all sorts of strange situations. Being succulent, they can handle drying out with ease, but they aren't like some dry-tolerant plants that collapse the moment they are too wet. They won't grow where they are constantly soggy and certainly prefer good drainage, but they're not drama queens about it, in most cases. The exception being extremely hairy "spiderweb" or "cobweb" forms which, like most very hairy plants, can be quite wet intolerant.

This lack of fussiness means semps are prime candidates for nontraditional containers. Old boots and shoes make happy homes for semps, as does just about anything else you can think of. Their dry tolerance makes them fine with the limited soil mass in these unusual planters, and they don't lose their cool if that old shoe doesn't drain perfectly after a rainstorm or watering either.

above › **An unnamed variegated semp in a Denver garden.**

right › **A nice red unnamed semp.**

Maybe it is the fact that they are so easy, so commonly traded around for free, or possibly that their history of living in old boots gives them an air of frivolity, but semps don't get much respect. Which is a shame. If only they were difficult, fussy, expensive, and only seen in the company of hand-carved stone troughs and the choicest of gentians, we'd have whole societies devoted to semps. They're evergreen, looking terrific absolutely all year, have beautifully varied, intricate geometric forms, leaves ranging from bright green to glaucous gray to dark purple-red, and of course the hairs, which go from the smooth to the softly fuzzy to the dramatic and unique long hairs of the spiderweb forms. Rosettes can be smaller than a fingernail or wider then your palm, and the flowers, though not often thought of as a feature, are rather attractive as well, in shades of yellow (often tinged green) to red.

Sempervivums not only have a great range of variation between the different varieties, but each individual plant can also be quite a chameleon, looking radically different in different conditions and times of the year. The amount of red in the leaves, for example, increases with more sun and cooler temperatures, and greens out in warmer, shadier conditions. Ultraviolet light is the main trigger for red pigment formation here (and with most

left › *Orostachys spinosa.*

above › **Happy semps in Paula Flynn's Iowa garden.**

plants), so in greenhouses (which screen out most of the UV rays) semps will be much greener than they would be in similar conditions outdoors. Water also has a big impact. Plants grown dry will form much smaller, tighter rosettes than those grown wet. Now, to be sure, essentially all plants will be smaller and tighter when grown on the dry side, but for semps the difference is particularly extreme; simply taking a dry plant and watering it can completely transform its overall look as the leaves plump up and expand. The difference is particularly striking with the spiderweb semps. When dry, the leaves pull in on themselves, pulling together the hairs of the "spiderweb" to make almost a solid white covering over the plant. Water thoroughly, and that very same plant will open up to a wide, green plant with just a light network of hairs over it. This is a wonderful adaptation, allowing the plant to photosynthesize when it has plenty of water, but then if it gets too dry, it is able to reflect away most of the sunlight to protect itself from drying out further.

Semps have a distinctive and unusual plan of growth. Each plant forms a large main rosette (the hen), and then grows out new side rosettes around it (the chicks). Those secondary rosettes expand to become new hens in

their own right, producing their own new chicks. Once a rosette reaches full size and maturity, it flowers, sending up an often quite tall spike of flowers, producing masses of seeds; it then expires, leaving the other rosettes to carry on.

Along with sempervivums, I lump the equally charming genus *Orostachys*. They have the same general growth habit, same easy-going disposition, and are just as worth including in your garden. Particularly look out for *Orostachys fimbriata*, with lovely brown leaves, and *Orostachys spinosa*, which has the handy trick of looking completely different every time of the year. It overwinters as a tight, tiny ball you can hardly see and expands to a very sempervivum-like rosette in spring. Over the course of the summer, it morphs into something that looks almost like a daisy, with a ring of long leaves on the outside and a flat, tight disk of short leaves in the center.

Tulips

Tulipa clusiana var. chrysantha brings bright glowing color to the spring garden.

When the big Dutch bulb catalogs come in the fall (or summer, it seems like they arrive earlier every year), their photos of enormous spreads of tall tulips in garish colors may seem like the total opposite of anything appropriate for the rock garden, but there are very good reasons to include tulips and many other "common" Dutch bulbs in the rock garden. Tulips, like many bulbs, are in fact superbly adapted to the good drainage and warm, sunny conditions of a rock garden. Tulips have evolved their peculiar life cycle—shooting into growth rapidly in the spring, then quickly retreating underground to wait out the summer and winter as a bulb—as an adaptation to the harsh conditions where they evolved, mostly in Turkey, where between hot dry summers and cold winters, the moist moderation of spring is the only time they can really do any growing. Having adapted to survive a brutally dry summer, a typi-cally wet, well-irrigated summer in the garden can be the kiss of death, or at least the start of a long,

left › **A
soft-yellow
form of** *Tulipa
batalinii.*

slow decline. But sitting in the well-drained gravel and sand of a rock garden, they'll thrive.

Though almost all tulips will thrive in rock garden conditions, aesthetically you'll probably want to keep away from the huge hybrid tulips with their massive flowers and tall stems, as they'll just look out of place. Instead, look to the species tulips and near-species hybrids, and you'll find a smaller stature and wilding grace perfectly suited to mingle with your drabas and dianthus. As an added bonus, while large hybrid tulips are short-lived in most climates, most of the species forms will not only perennialize, but also multiply into larger drifts every year.

Consider, in particular, the selections of *Tulipa batalinii*, which has narrow, gray leaves and luminous flowers in shades of yellow, orange, or red; or the slim, elegant blooms of *T. clusiana*, each petal either (depending on the form) white or yellow with a stripe of red down the middle. Or the

above › *Tulipa* 'Little Princess' blooming beside a daphne at Broadleigh Gardens.

lovely selection 'Little Princess', which has small cup-shaped flowers that open to bright stars with a dramatic color scheme of orange centered with yellow, and in the very center a dark, almost black eye.

And while you are shopping for species tulips, throw in a few miniature daffodils or species crocuses. They may not be rare or unusual, but they'll thrive in rock garden conditions and you'll be very happy to see them every spring.

Metric Conversions

INCHES	CM
½	1.3
1	2.5
2	5.1
3	7.6
4	10
5	13
6	15
7	18
8	20
9	23
10	25
20	51
30	76
40	100
50	130

FEET	M
1	0.3
2	0.6
3	0.9
4	1.2
5	1.5
6	1.8
7	2.1
8	2.4
9	2.7
10	3
20	6
30	9

TEMPERATURES

$$°C = 5/9 \times (°F - 32)$$

$$°F = (9/5 \times °C) + 32$$

Alpine Resources

Mail order nurseries in North America

Alplains
(seed only)
alplains.com

Arrowhead Alpines
arrowheadalpines.com

Edelweiss Perennials
edelweissperennials.com

High Country Gardens
highcountrygardens.com

Mountain Crest Gardens
mountaincrestgardens.com

Siskiyou Rare Plant Nursery
siskiyourareplantnursery.com

Sunscapes Rare Plant Nursery
sunscapes.net

Wild Ginger Farm
wildgingerfarm.com

Wrightman Alpines
wrightmanalpines.com

Nurseries in the United Kingdom

Ardfearn Nursery
ardfearn-nursery.co.uk

Ashwood Nursery
ashwoodnurseries.com

Border Alpines
borderalpines.co.uk

D'Arcy & Everest
darcyeverest.co.uk

Hartside Garden Nursery
plantswithaltitude.co.uk

Kevlock Garden Plants
kevlockgarden.co.uk

MacPlants
Macplants.co.uk

Mendle Nursery
Mendlenursery.co.uk

Plants for Small Gardens
Plantsforsmallgardens.co.uk

Pottertons Nursery
Pottertons.co.uk

Slack Top Alpines
Slacktopnurseries.co.uk

Timpany Nurseries and Gardens
Timpanynurseries.com

Rock garden societies

North American Rock Garden Society
nargs.org

Alpine Garden Society
alpinegardensociety.net

Scottish Rock Garden Club
srgc.net

Further Reading

Calvo, Janit. 2013. *Gardening in Miniature: Create Your Own Tiny Living World*. Portland, OR: Timber Press.

Charlesworth, Geoffrey B. 1988. *The Opinionated Gardener: Random Offshoots from an Alpine Garden*. Boston, MA: David R. Godine, Publisher.

Farrer, Reginald. 1913. *The English Rock-Garden*. London: England: T.C. & E.C. Jack, Ltd.

Grey-Wilson, Christopher, ed. 1989. *A Manual of Alpine and Rock Garden Plants*. Portland, OR: Timber Press.

Korn, Peter. 2013. *Peter Korn's Garden: Giving Plants What They Want*. Molndal, Sweden: Peter Korn.

McGary, Jane, ed. 2003. *Rock Garden Design and Construction*. Portland, OR: Timber Press.

McGregor, Malcolm. 2008. *Saxifrages: A Definitive Guide to the 2000 Species, Hybrids, and Cultivars*. Portland, OR: Timber Press.

Norris, Nancy. 2011. *Miniature Garden Guidebook: For Beautiful Rock Gardens, Container Plantings, Bonsai, Garden Railways*. Waukesha, WI: Kalmbach Publishing.

Acknowledgments

Thanks to all the brilliant gardeners whose so generously not only allowed me to visit their gardens, ask them questions, and take loads of pictures, but also often fed me lunch or dinner or offered me a place to stay and then took time out of their busy lives to drive me all over creation to show me other remarkable gardens in their area, shared photos I needed at the last minute, and answered desperate e-mails when I was searching for the missing name of a plant, gardener, or garden, and, most of all, sent me home with plants in my luggage. Gardeners the world over are a huge, plant-obsessed, generous extended family to me, and I couldn't have come close to creating this book without their generosity throughout my gardening life.

Equal thanks to the talented editors at Timber Press who deal with and fix my sloppy writing and constant questions.

All these talented people are responsible for anything good about this book. Any errors (and I'm sure there are many) I fully intend to blame on my cat, Mohanty. He's very cute. He also likes to walk on keyboards.

Photography Credits

Bobby J. Ward, pages 36 top, 38 right, 40, 41, 147

Cliff Booker, pages 90, 92, 93, 95

Glenn Shapiro, pages 44 bottom left, 50, 51, 250, 264, 265

Janit Calvo, page 113

Michael Shadrack, pages 226, 227, 228

Mike Kintgen, pages 52, 54, 56, 58

Saxon Holt, page 11 right

GAP Photos Ltd.

Annie Green-Armytage, page 138 top

Carole Drake, pages 94, 134–135

Clive Nichols, page 154

Dianna Jazwinski, page 172

Elke Borkowski, pages 108, 145 right

FhF Greenmedia, page 213

Gary Smith, pages 2, 6

Hanneke Reijbroek, page 128

Howard Rice, page 116 top

J S Sira, page 22

Jenny Lilly, photographer; Jade Goto and Armando Raish, design, page 100

Jerry Harpur, page 116 bottom

John Glover, pages 4, 104

John Swithinbank, page 127

Jonathan Buckley, pages 10 bottom, 194

Jonathan Need, page 10 top

Marion Brenner, page 83

Martin Staffler, pages 214 top, 256

Michael Howes, photographer; RHS Hampton Court Palace Flower Show 2011, Hopleys, Much Hadham, Herts, page 182

Nicola Stocken, pages 96, 137

Pernilla Bergdahl, page 88

Richard Bloom, page 246

Rob Whitworth, page 240

Thomas Alamy, page 148

Tim Gainey, page 139

Flickr

Used under a Creative Commons Attribution 2.0 Generic license

Andrey Zharkikh, page 242

Caroline, page 185

Jürgen und Susanne Lohr, page 223

Maja Dumat, page 222

Mount Rainier National Park, page 241

Used under a Creative Commons Attribution–Share Alike 2.0 Generic license

Udo Schmidt, page 184

Wikimedia Commons

Used under a Creative Commons Attribution–Share Alike 3.0 Unported license

Averater, page 214 bottom

Used under a Creative Commons Attribution–Share Alike 4.0 International license

Isidre blanc, page 258 bottom

Index

Joseph Tychonievich studied horticulture, plant breeding, and genetics at the Ohio State University and was the nursery manager at Arrowhead Alpines, a premier rock garden nursery in Fowlerville, Michigan. He spent a summer working at Shibamichi Honten Nursery in Japan and has been a repeat guest on the public radio food show *The Splendid Table*.

Starting from the age of five when he asked his parents for seeds for his birthday, Joseph has had a deep and abiding obsession with just about everything photosynthetic, from the vegetable garden to the rock garden. *Organic Gardening Magazine* called him one of "six young horticulturists who are helping to shape how America gardens." His other book is *Plant Breeding for the Home Gardener: How to Create Unique Vegetables and Flowers.*

Page 2: Dianthus, campanulas, and other alpines filling a rock garden with spring color.
Page 4: Saxifrages in full bloom in a small crevice garden.

Published in 2016 by Timber Press
The Haseltine Building
133 S.W. Second Avenue, Suite 450
Portland, Oregon 97204-3527
timberpress.com

Printed in China
Text design by Stacy Wakefield Forte
Cover design by Adrianna Sutton

Library of Congress Cataloging-in-Publication Data

Names: Tychonievich, Joseph, author.
Title: Rock gardening : reimagining a classic style / Joseph
    Tychonievich.
Description: Portland, Oregon : Timber Press, Inc., 2016. | Includes
  bibliographical references and index.
Identifiers: LCCN 2016009686 | ISBN 9781604695878 (hardcover)
Subjects: LCSH: Rock gardens. | Rock plants.
Classification: LCC SB459.T93 2016 | DDC 635.9/672—dc23 LC
    record available at https://lccn.loc.gov/2016009686

A catalog record for this book is also available from the British Library.